CAMBRIDGE LIBRARY COLLECTION

Books of enduring scholarly value

Archaeology

The discovery of material remains from the recent or the ancient past has always been a source of fascination, but the development of archaeology as an academic discipline which interpreted such finds is relatively recent. It was the work of Winckelmann at Pompeii in the 1760s which first revealed the potential of systematic excavation to scholars and the wider public. Pioneering figures of the nineteenth century such as Schliemann, Layard and Petrie transformed archaeology from a search for ancient artifacts, by means as crude as using gunpowder to break into a tomb, to a science which drew from a wide range of disciplines - ancient languages and literature, geology, chemistry, social history - to increase our understanding of human life and society in the remote past.

Accidents of an Antiquary's Life

The archaeologist D. G. Hogarth (1862–1927) was, when he died, keeper of the Ashmolean Museum and president of the Royal Geographical Society, whose gold medal he was also awarded. This 1910 book is his account of various episodes in his career from 1897, when he covered the Cretan revolt against Turkey for *The Times*, to his 1907 excavations in Asyut, Egypt. A mixture of travel writing and archaeological reporting – the volume also contains an academic report on the excavation of Carchemish – this book, a follow-up to his *A Wandering Scholar in the Levant* (also reissued in this series), and intended for a popular audience, remains a highly readable account of the practicalities behind Hogarth's intellectual career. It also provides background to Hogarth's political involvement with the Near East, as acting director of the Arab Bureau in Cairo during the First World War and an attendee at the Versailles peace conference.

Cambridge University Press has long been a pioneer in the reissuing of out-of-print titles from its own backlist, producing digital reprints of books that are still sought after by scholars and students but could not be reprinted economically using traditional technology. The Cambridge Library Collection extends this activity to a wider range of books which are still of importance to researchers and professionals, either for the source material they contain, or as landmarks in the history of their academic discipline.

Drawing from the world-renowned collections in the Cambridge University Library, and guided by the advice of experts in each subject area, Cambridge University Press is using state-of-the-art scanning machines in its own Printing House to capture the content of each book selected for inclusion. The files are processed to give a consistently clear, crisp image, and the books finished to the high quality standard for which the Press is recognised around the world. The latest print-on-demand technology ensures that the books will remain available indefinitely, and that orders for single or multiple copies can quickly be supplied.

The Cambridge Library Collection brings back to life books of enduring scholarly value (including out-of-copyright works originally issued by other publishers) across a wide range of disciplines in the humanities and social sciences and in science and technology.

Accidents of an Antiquary's Life

D. G. HOGARTH

CAMBRIDGE UNIVERSITY PRESS

Cambridge, New York, Melbourne, Madrid, Cape Town,
Singapore, São Paolo, Delhi, Tokyo, Mexico City

Published in the United States of America by Cambridge University Press, New York

www.cambridge.org
Information on this title: www.cambridge.org/9781108041928

This edition first published 1920
This digitally printed version 2012

ISBN 978-1-108-04192-8 Paperback

ACCIDENTS OF AN ANTIQUARY'S LIFE

MACMILLAN AND CO., LIMITED
LONDON BOMBAY · CALCUTTA
MELBOURNE

THE MACMILLAN COMPANY
NEW YORK · BOSTON · CHICAGO
ATLANTA · SAN FRANCISCO

THE MACMILLAN CO. OF CANADA, LTD.
TORONTO

FRENCH CORPORAL DRILLING CRETAN VILLAGE GUARDS (1898).

Frontispiece.

ACCIDENTS

OF AN

ANTIQUARY'S LIFE

BY

D. G. HOGARTH

AUTHOR OF 'A WANDERING SCHOLAR,' ETC.

WITH FORTY ILLUSTRATIONS
FROM PHOTOGRAPHS TAKEN BY THE AUTHOR
AND HIS COMPANIONS

MACMILLAN AND CO., LIMITED
ST. MARTIN'S STREET, LONDON
1910

GLASGOW: PRINTED AT THE UNIVERSITY PRESS
BY ROBERT MACLEHOSE AND CO. LTD.

PREFACE

AMONG many companions in these accidents who are not named in the text, lest the book should become a string of names, I have to thank five especially because they have allowed me to use photographs taken when we were together. These are Mr. Alison V. Armour, owner of the "Utowana," Mr. Richard Norton, a comrade during the cruise of that yacht and at Siut and in Syria, Messrs. A. W. Van Buren and C. D. Curtis, members of the yachting party, and Mr. J. A. R. Munro, who endured many things with me in Asia Minor in 1891. Four others, Dr. A. C. Headlam, who was the third of Sir W. M. Ramsay's party in 1890, Mr. B. Christian, my companion in Thessaly before the Graeco-Turkish war broke out, Mr. J. G. C. Anderson, who cruised with me to Lycia in 1897, and Mr. A. E. Henderson, who did loyal service at Ephesus, I cannot forbear to name. I have also to express thanks to the proprietors and editors of three magazines, the *Monthly*, *Cornhill*, and *Macmillan's*, for their kind consent to my using, in five chapters of this book, the second to the sixth, parts of articles which appeared in their issues prior to 1905. Finally, my friend and critic, Charles Robert Leslie Fletcher, who read this book in proof, knows how greatly I am beholden to him.

D. G. H.

OXFORD, 1909.

CONTENTS

LIST OF ILLUSTRATIONS

INTRODUCTORY.

APOLOGY OF AN APPRENTICE.

> And ta'en the—*Antiquarian trade*
> I think they call it.
>
> *Burns.*

I WILL not take the name of Antiquary without apology, and hereby, *liberandi animam meam causa*, make it in an Introductory, to be passed over if the reader pleases. Your true Antiquary is born, not made. Sometimes an infirmity or awkwardness of body, which has disposed a boy to shun the pursuits of his fellows, may help to detach the man for the study of forgotten far off things; but it is essential that there be inborn in him the type of mind which is more curious of the past than the present, loves detail for its own sake, and cares less for ends than means.

Nevertheless, accident may make an Antiquary, as good as another, out of anybody whose boyish education has given him, willy nilly, some knowledge of the elder world. Let him be thrown, for example, in early manhood, much into lands whose ancient monuments conspicuously exalt the past at the expense of the present. The necessary curiosity can grow within him, disposing his mind to study antiquarian detail as a duty, and, in time, a pleasure; and through apprenticeship he may learn and love the trade to which he was not born.

I claim to be no better than this Antiquary made, and made none too soon. Nothing disposed me to the trade in early years. If I was taken as a child to minsters and abbeys, I endured their chill aisles in lively hope of a pastrycook to come, and at our oldest Public School had no feeling for the grey Gothic austerities among which live the Foundationers, of whose number I was not. Nor was it until half my Oxford course had been run that I discovered curiosity about any ancient thing, and that curiosity was far from antiquarian. Scholar of my College though I was, I had been better known as a freshman for a gamester in a small way than for anything else; but some study was forced upon me, and in the course of it I happened on Mommsen's panegyric of Caesar. The charm of guessing ancient motives from the records of ancient deeds fascinated me—there is much in the pursuit to appeal to a gambler—and I resolved to attempt a speculative biography of some great man. Looking about me for another imperial figure, I fixed, greatly daring, on Alexander the Great, foreswore cards and the course, and stepped out of the strict lists of the schools into the field of Macedonian history. The spacious world over which Alexander moved fired my imagination and stirred a lust for discovery. As a child my keenest joy was to announce the finding of an untrodden way in the outskirts of a Lincolnshire townlet, and my best remembered grief was to learn that it was already known and named.

I could write a good deal about Macedonians when I went into the Schools, but barely enough on other matters to win salvation; and if I was made presently a tutor and fellow of my College, it was less for my actual scholarship than for hope of its future. I found academic life not greatly to my liking at that age, and when an endowment for scholarly travel abroad was set for competition, I entered in forlorn hope of escape. To the equal surprise of others, I was chosen among better scholars, and found myself in a quandary. If I was to research abroad as a classical scholar, I wished to explore Alexander's steps; but to go up alone into Asia was beyond my means. A friend, who knew my difficulty, told me that William Martin Ramsay, the well-known traveller in Asia Minor, needed an apprentice. Asia Minor was not Persia, but it was Asia, and fair field for a pioneer. I offered myself, and was accepted, but on the sole condition, that I made some preliminary study at the newly-founded Archaeological School in Athens. I knew nothing of Greek archaeology, having never during six years entered the Museum of my own Oxford; and thus, at an age when most archaeologists are past masters of some branch of their trade, I had to begin apprenticeship. Perhaps it may interest some to hear by what accidents an antiquary of a sort was made out of a wandering scholar.

I went to Athens early in 1887, as raw a neophyte as ever entered Academe. The British School, then in its first youth, was not yet assured of its place in the local republic of science, and held little converse with other Schools. The famous Antiquary who directed it could have guided better, though not more gladly, a student of Attic architecture than a would-be explorer of Asia, and the library held few books, though, heaven knows, enough that I had not read. My one fellow-student helped me much, and would have helped me more, had I been in the temper to learn. But I had come to Athens as a man should not, if he is to love her—come without trained taste for the ancient art, which is her only wealth, and without instinctive reverence for her soil. I gaped at her monuments like any other tourist, though with less than the common understanding, fled from German lectures on her topography, and took refuge in studying her inscriptions as students of history will who are brought unworthy into the presence of her art. For pastime, beside visiting a few neighbouring spots of which I knew not enough to find them interesting, I roamed mean streets and dusty suburbs, regretting the world I had left, and longing for another in the east, with a prospect of Asiatic travel for my sole comfort.

Two months passed drearily, and I escaped to Macedonia. The rickety vessel broke down for the third time at the second sunrise, and, wakened by the stoppage, I climbed sleepily on deck to find myself in a world of fog. A sudden gleam pierced the mist: I turned to see a patch of heaven, and in it, immeasurably high, one hard rose-red cloud. "*Olympe!*" said a deck hand. The peak stood revealed a moment only; but I had seen the seat of the Gods.

Salonica, *sale unique*, as the skipper punned, received me for ten days, and, with its camel-trains and Jews, black-bearded and cruel-eyed as men that kill prophets offered a foretaste of the East. It was in days before the railway had come down the Vardar valley and before the Great Fire, and the town, packed more close than now into its frame of white wall, was more odorous, less Italianized, less passable. Under the aegis of a Turk-loving Consul I hunted inscriptions in alleys and courts and stone-cutters' yards and the purlieus of an unreformed *konak*, and, beginning to feel the explorer's itch, would go up to Vodhena to find what might be left of Aegae;

but Consul and Pasha forbade lest another Briton be captured by the bands that had taken Synge and Souttar. I was too innocent then to discount official fears, still believing, indeed, that one should walk, revolver on hip, even in Salonica streets; and in the end I proposed no more than to drive to the site of Pella. I went off with a young consular assistant and a guard, rumbling along, gensdarmes to right and gensdarmes to left, as I should never journey again in Turkey. There were soldiers at the coffee-halts, soldiers at the *khans*, soldiers guarding the bridge which crossed the slow-turning eddies of the Vardar, and soldiers holding Yenije, where astute bugs, who found saucers of water barring their usual access, painfully climbed the leprous walls and dropped from ceiling to pillow. The Yenije gravestones are mostly blocks brought from Pella, and on the site of the ancient city itself lie others, with two fragments of fluted Doric shafts, near a fountain still called Pel. For the rest, Pella has vanished as though it had never been. Out of dusty undulating fields; out of half a dozen barrows; out of a low marshy plain to west and south; out of a glorious horseshoe of hills with the snowy saddle of Olympus at one horn—out of these you must conjure your vision of Philip's home.

It was the middle of May when I was free of Athens, and, passing over to Smyrna, found Ramsay about to start. A third member of the party arrived two days later, an adventurous fellow who had spent part of his youth in Albania and Montenegro, and, knowing little of ancient things, cared less, so he had a good horse to ride and an unknown track to follow. The apparatus of travel, which we gathered at Smyrna, was of the simplest,—a single tent and a few pots and pans, but no canned stores; and two simple villagers were hired to serve us. The qualifications of the one chosen to cook became manifest on the second night in camp. We had left railhead at Seraikeuy, and ridden up the Lycus valley to the foot of the white cliffs of Hierapolis. Mehmet bought a turkey of the peasants of Pambuk Kalessi, and was bidden to have it ready for the next night's supper. Early on the morrow we went up to the site, and all that day, under a broiling sun and among some of the best preserved Roman tombs in Asia Minor, I entered on an arduous apprenticeship to the best epigraphist in Europe. Sharpset at nightfall we hurried down expectant of our turkey. Mehmet sat placid, the bird at his feet. It was a corpse, indeed, but no more, not even a plucked one. "What am I to do with this"? said Mehmet.

He learned better as time went on; but throughout that journey we had little except sodden messes to eat, faring worse than any traveller need fare. It was partly because our leader cared little what he ate, but more because, like his followers, he journeyed on a slender purse. Ramsay had made to himself a European reputation as an explorer of Asia Minor at a cost which another man would think scarcely sufficient for the tour of Germany; and it had become his principle, as, for similar reasons it has become Petrie's, to suffer none but the barest means to his end. If both have pushed their practice to exceeding discomfort, both have taught several young Britons how little is necessity and how much superfluity: and it is not the least of my many debts to Ramsay that I gained in my first tour of exploration the will and the capacity to go farther at less cost than perhaps anyone but my master.

THE WHITE CLIFFS OF HIERAPOLIS.

Facing p. 6.

This part of my education had begun at once: for while we were still in Smyrna, Ramsay, wanting information about two sites lying north of the Aidin railway, had suggested that I should visit them alone, all raw as I was, and rejoin him at railhead. Feeling like a boy packed off to his first school, I agreed, and took the train to Nazli. I knew very little Greek, and less Turkish, but the Nazli stationmaster, christened Achilles, was reported to speak my tongue. He so far justified his fame as to greet me, stranded forlorn on the tracks, with "How you do, my boy?" When my Oxford manner had readjusted itself, we conversed sufficiently in French; and he found me a dancing stallion and sent me off astride a deep and angular military saddle with my knees level with my hips, the centre of a curvetting escort of the youth of Nazli. My first site proved to be a large hillock once surrounded by walls, and still bearing ruins of Roman baths, towards which an aqueduct straggled across the valley. It certainly looked like the ancient Mastaura which I had come out to see; and all doubt was soon settled by an inscription of that town which, on my return, I found built into a church wall at Nazli, and copied as best I might. After a sleepless night, stiff, sore, and with less skin than had left Smyrna, I went to the second site, and thence, proud but thankful, took train to railhead.

When our modest caravan had left Hierapolis, it wandered awhile on either bank of the upper Maeander, sometimes dropping a thousand feet to the stream, but for the most part keeping the high ground. The land flowed with milk and honey if not much else, and I learned the grave courtesy of the Anatolian peasant.

Twice we were called to shelter from the noonday sun in the portico of a mosque, and whatever the *ayan*, patron of strangers in that ordered village society, could procure of the best, was set before us. Our main purpose was to find inscriptions, and I was taught by precept and example how a villager may be induced to guide an inquisitive *giaur* into the recesses of his *haremlik*, or grub up the headstone of his forefather, or even saw away the floor of his mosque. But it was not always plain sailing; and how we used the wisdom of the serpent, and what reward was ours at one Maeander village, Badinlar, I have told already in another book.

I soon became interested in the simple arts of antiquarian travel, the seeking, the copying, the noting, the measuring, and the mapping, but it was some time before I could practise them in any comfort. The food or the climate, or both, caused at the first severe saddle-boils, for whose easing there were no long halts. To a rider in such plight it means much if his horse trip on stony tracks, lash out at his fellow, plunge and burst his girths in a bog, incontinently roll on a chance sandpatch, or calmly sit down in a ford to cool his haunches. A sorry steed, bought in my innocence at eight pounds English, and dear at two, introduced me to each and all of these packhorse tricks. But the spacious landscapes, the dry warm airs, the novelty of man, beast, bird and flower, kept me going; and was I not in the land where I would be?

A chance visit to Sandukli brought me into my earliest collision with Ottoman authority. It was in the hungry month of Ramazan, and two of us had ridden in from camp to buy what supplies we might in the early hours of morning. As we were about remounting, the police accosted us, and roughly bade us wait on the governor. Led to the *konak*, we were told his beyship was abed, and we must stay till he had eaten at sundown. To spend a whole day in dusty Sandukli was bad, but worse to spend it waiting on a Bey's pleasure. We sent word that we gave him half an hour to appear, and, admired by all the loafers of the *bazar*, stalked up and down, watch in hand, in all the insolence of Britain abroad. The governor came not, but on the call of time sent a deputy, nervously offering excuse, and begging us go in peace. Ours is not a gracious race, but it usually gets what it wants.

Passing north-eastward through Afium Kara Hissar in mid June, we went up to our goal in the Phrygian Monument country, and for all the rest of the month were busied in exploring its pleasant shaggy valleys and carven cliffs. I have seen since no region so thickly set with strange memorials of the past, and none to which I would more joyfully return. Some day when diggers uncover the relics of that Midaean monarchy which seemed to the early Greeks of Asia the eldest and most god-like of powers, may I be there to see! The haunted valley of Ayazin, where we grubbed mole-like under the face of a fallen tomb, and, prone in the shallow pit we had made, sketched the most curious of Phrygian reliefs: the sheer acropolis of Kumbet, where we planned a mysterious rock-house which may be of any antiquity; the gorges of Bakshish and Yapuldak, whose sculptured tombs, fashioned like houses of the living, are seen suddenly through the pines: that stupendous curtain of carved and written stone hung before the gate of death by which Midas the King passed to the Great Mother; all his desolate, impregnable city above it, with inscribed altars and rock-reliefs—of these is woven my "*fèerie du premier voyage*." I was the photographer of the expedition, equipped with a camera which I had borrowed of an amateur in Smyrna and manipulated for the space of one afternoon under his patient eye—so unready was I for my trade; and I was an assistant surveyor, who having plotted painfully and with many lapses my half of the fortifications of the Midas City, was well enough satisfied with my botched work to question my master's survey of the other half. He has long forgiven me.

A strenuous and somewhat nervous week we spent there under the Midaean crags. Unwarned of modern tenants, we found a new settlement of Circassians, who in those days had a bad name all over Asia Minor for a certain lawless truculence, born of pride of race, and fostered by the official perfidy with which they were often treated. But Mehmet Bey, the chief, received us cordially with *samovar* and smooth words. On the morrow he followed our operations among the monuments with very lively interest, and at evening came down to the camp and roundly proposed to share profits. We told him once and again there was no gold in our hopes; but we talked to deaf ears, and at last, to be rid of him, said we would halve such treasure as we might find. This, we well knew, was to sow trouble for early reaping, in a land where all believe that the Frank spirits bullion out of earth and rocks, though one see it ever so little; and we were not comforted by our muleteers' tales of a recent killing, for which the Ottoman government was holding Mehmet Bey to account. But the local police, who had kept track of us, summoned the Bey to Karahissar on the third day, and thus nothing worse befell than a cooling of cordiality between camp and village as the days went by without our doing anything but draw lines on paper and squint through sights.

When, at last, we had done what we came to do, we thought it well to ride fast and far, almost to Karahissar again. Thereafter we became two bands, Ramsay making for home, and his two scholars setting forth for the Cilician shore with no more baggage than might be carried on their saddle-horses and a third bestridden by a single servant. How first one of us and then the other fell ill, but neither so ill as he thought; what in our ignorance and inexperience we did and saw; how we came over Taurus in a waggon and took ship, I have already told elsewhere.

I did not return to Asia for three years, though within a twelvemonth I was wandering within sight of her snows. I had gone to Cyprus as one of four to dig, and I stayed alone to travel during the torrid summer of 1888, visiting almost every village of the island, and trying to do, with not half his science, what I had seen my master do on my prentice journey. What indeed I did do I wrote in a book, little known and less read, whose title, *Devia Cypria*, has deceived more than once, I am told, sanguine buyers of Erotica. Of the part I bore in the excavation of Paphos I will say little. I knew nothing of the digger's art at the beginning, and very little at the end. Our leader had studied in the Egyptian school of Petrie, but the rest of us were so raw as not to know if there were any science of the spade at all. We had for mentor Gregori of Larnaca, who has become more famous since, and I doubt if we did much harm. But I doubt too if we found nearly all we ought to have found on that immemorial site. Some experience in handling unskilled Greeks, a fluent use of their rustic tongue, an inkling of how much I had to learn—this, however, I took away from Paphos.

Less than two years later I was with Ramsay in Asia again. The railhead of the Aidin line had been pushed in the meantime to Dineir, and we could make our start from far inland. It is often disputed which of two courses be best, to buy transport or to hire. The hirer must wrangle morning and night with muleteers, who use every trick of their trade to shorten and ease the day's work. The buyer will be cheated when he buys, cheated when he feeds, cheated when he sells again, and he takes all risk of horse thieves. Our lot on this journey was rare and happy. The animals we had were none of ours; but their owner, unwilling to take the road, sent a Greek hireling in his stead. A month later, after many bickerings and a final fight with his Moslem fellows, the Christian took to his heels, leaving his master's horses on our hands. Quit of responsibility we rode them other three months from one end of Asia Minor to the other, and though the two best were lifted by Circassians at a late stage of the journey, the owner, advised long ago of his hireling's flight, was so amazed to see any beasts of his again, that, as we told their hire into his hand, he refrained himself from cursing and blessed us for honest men.

We rode off into the hills of Pisidia to pick up inscriptions here and there, but more often to revise texts that Ramsay had seen in earlier years. There were few or no adventures to vary the daily round of a copyist, cynosure of an adhesive crowd in graveyards, or desired of raging dogs in the houses and courts. One noon the sun was eclipsed, and, at the moment of deepest shadow, we rode nervously into a remote village to find ourselves neither incensed for gods nor stoned for devils, but wholly neglected for the heavenly phenomenon, which was being calmly observed through smoked glass.

By the lovely lake of Egerdir came a fever-fiend to try the first of many bouts with me. It was a malign freak of fortune. Our waggon, with all baggage and medical comforts, had been sent by ferry across the lake to a point where, by riding round the southern bight, we might meet it on the second day; but failing to pass a rocky ridge, it fetched a wide compass to the north and made for another goal beyond the mountains. My fever began on the first afternoon, and sitting like a sack on a tired horse, with a sense of dull blows falling on the nape of my neck, I followed the pack-train till dusk up a wild valley where was said to be a hamlet. It proved ruinous and void, and almost supperless we had to pass the chill night in the open, lying on the soil with saddles under our heads. It sounds a romantic bivouac; but in sober fact a saddle that has clung to a hot and ill-groomed horse for a summer's day makes a very sorry pillow: and lift stones as you may from the bosom of mother earth, she will privily thrust up as many more against your salient parts all the uneasy night.

Next morning we were away betimes, but doomed to wander for many hours behind ignorant or knavish guides in tangles of the Pisidian hills, I slaking an insatiate thirst at every torrent and spring. It was nightfall when we reached the bourne of our journey, the site of Adada at Kara Baulo, whose modern name must survive from some church of Paul the Apostle, built perhaps in commemoration of a halt made by the first mission to the Gentiles on its way from Perga of Pamphylia to Pisidian Antioch. There I slept once more on mother earth under the stars, having supped, loathing, on broth in which floated shell-less unborn eggs. On the morrow I could do little but lie in the shade, while the rest explored the forest-girt ruins: but by noon their work was done, and I had to mount and follow to a hamlet in a low pass above the Eurymedon gorge. We lodged in a shed, and I read in my diary "cold and very lumpy lying." The fourth stage, over nine hours long, took us across Eurymedon and up towards the snow-streaked crest of Anamás Dagh; for on we had to press for fear our waggoners should give us up for lost and trundle back to Dineir. Night found us lying on naked rock within a low circle of rough stones near an Alpine *yaila* or summer camp. We had been fed by the hospitable shepherds and given screens of felt against the bitter wind; but fever and its ague pains shooting through loins and legs banished sleep, and I sat up or paced till dawn.

At sunrise a peasant offered to show a painted cave, and hearing it was but a step along the hillside I offered to visit it. On we trudged; farther fled the cave; and not until the best part of an hour had passed were we halted before the mouth of a mean little Byzantine shrine. The sun was already high, and the morning windless. Bathed in sweat I scarcely dragged myself back over the rough path, and reached camp with a livid face. My companions lifted me into the saddle and hurried me across the pass, doubting, as they told me later, if I should live to taste quinine again. But as the day wore on, the fever began to abate. The sweat under the early sun had broken it, and I was in a fair way to be cured, not killed, when we found the waggon awaiting us at the edge of the eastern plain.

I remained weak, however, and altogether indifferent to the work I had to do. Two years before, while alone in Cyprus, I had thought myself an antiquary, who explored ancient things for the love of science. Now I found them infinitely tedious, and moodily confessed I was no antiquary yet, not even a wandering scholar, but just a hunter at hazard. I did what my master wished of me: but my interest was in matters outside his work, in the incidents of the camp, in the means of travel, in the wildness of nature and man about us, in the beauty of the Beysheher lake seen through mist from a hill-top one morning, in the old boar, whom I flushed, as I was scrambling down again, and blessed that he did not charge. We went down from Konia into Cilicia, and in the hot valley of the Calycadnus and hotter coastlands near the Corycian Cave, where we were fain to sit in the pungent smoke of dung to escape worse torture of mosquitoes, my ill humour grew and I hated life until we doubled back to the heights, and the last memory of fever left me on the table-land of Kaisariyeh.

One of the party tarried with the American missionaries at Talas to recover of a worse Job's plague than had vexed me three years before, while Ramsay took me over Anti-Taurus to copy the Hittite inscriptions of Gurun. Some of the incidents of this journey I have told already, especially the buying of the Bor Stone and its sequel; and other incidents must remain untold here if I am to make an end of these early wanderings. Sufficient to say that after we had recrossed Anti-Taurus, where boars came grunting one night almost to the camp-fires, which shone on their watering-place, and after we had discovered the Hittite relief of Fraktin, I left Ramsay to go home with the waggon, and, joined by the sick man from Kaisariyeh half cured but wholly undeterred, passed beneath the mighty wall of Ala Dagh to the foothills of Taurus. With the Hittite inscription of Bulgar Maden (how ill I copied it!) and the lower half of the Bor Stone to our credit, we set our faces homeward over the great Plains. On Dindymus I took a second fever of the kind that swells the limbs, and was brought by my comrade very sick to the railway and Dineir again.

This was to be the end of my apprenticeship in archaeological travel to the man who has made it a science. I was to have met Ramsay again in Cilicia the following year; but it was late in June before, scarcely recovered from another fever caught in Salonica, I landed at Mersina to find he had fled the coming heat. So I had to organize my own train and go up across the steaming Aleian plain to the Taurus with one companion, a traveller of infinite patience, as he had need to be that year. For little but mishap and delay was in store for us.

The first fortnight went well enough. We passed the mountains by way of the robber town of Hajin, where we spent a pleasant evening with two American mission ladies, who were to be caught by Kurds a week later, robbed, stripped, and lashed to trees: and near Comana we set ourselves to our first serious task, the tracing of the great military road which Severus made under the northward face of Taurus from Caesarea Mazaca to the standing camp of the "Thundering" Legion at Melitene. By the ruin of its embankment lie milestones of some ten Emperors, in groups of five or six, which Gregori, whom I had picked up in Cyprus, taught the peasants to lever over so we might read their inscriptions. Missing at every mile Ramsay's skill in decipherment and his knowledge of things Roman, we did what we could to unravel the tangled epigraphs—a rude week's work which left us little to learn about Roman milestones, and able to write a report which would win the heart of Mommsen.

The task was done at last at Arabissus, and we could turn off to Albistan to see a Hittite obelisk, and thence strike southward through Taurus, by way of stubborn Zeitun, to Marash in Commagene, where misfortune lay in wait. The Hittite stones which we had come down to see had been spirited away (I was not to see them till many years later in New York), and before we could fly the July heat of Syria, I was badly hurt by a fall, and laid on my back in a kindly missionary's house for two long weeks—a martyrdom of idleness for my luckless comrade. Then came cholera, raiding north from Aleppo, and thinking we might yet escape the quarantine cordon on the northern frontier of the province, we bolted through Taurus again, though I was still unable to walk. I had a nightmare ride up and down the rock ladders of the Pyramus gorge, my throbbing ankle supported on an improvised crutch; nor did time pass more gratefully for the companionship of an ill-looking Armenian doctor, whom we had been begged to take under our wing. Accused (falsely, we were told) of illicit commerce with a patient, he went in fear of his life from two Circassian bravos set by her brothers on his track, and we could not refuse to shield him; but I have heard since that he deserved whatever fate he escaped. And after all the cordon caught us and bade us camp on a bare hillside a few miles south of Derendeh for six torrid days till our captors' eyes could be opened (or closed) by practical but gentle methods of suasion. Not that the delay was time all lost; we passed on with my ankle almost sound, and another Hittite inscription added to our bag.

In Sivas it was my companion's turn to fall sick, and summer was far gone before we could enter on the last stage. We rode up the Halys valley to Zara and the scene of Pompey's victory at Nicopolis, and having turned thence down the course of the Pontic Lycus, through a pleasant Swiss region of pine forests and pine huts, inhabited by Shiahs, kindly to the *giaur* because despised by Sunnis for "red-head" heretics, came to the Black Sea by way of Neocaesarea and Comana Pontica and the Iris valley and Amasia and the baths of Phazemon. By the way we picked up some unconsidered trifles of Roman milestones and landmarks of Imperial Estates and the like, which we put on record long ago in a publication of the Royal Geographical Society; and from first to last, when not on the track of Hittites, we seemed to be following the footsteps of Rome. What has happened to the records of Persian and Greek dominion in Cappadocia? The Hittite and the Roman alone have set their marks on the rocks.

When I went back to Oxford I had some claim to

THE VALLEY OF THE PONTIC LYCUS AT SUNRISE.

Facing p. 18.

be a wandering scholar, but less to be an archaeological digger than was credited by those who asked me two years later to take charge of excavations promoted by the Egypt Exploration Fund. I ought not to have agreed, but, having so agreed, because the call of the East compelled me, I should have begun humbly at the bottom of the long ladder of Egyptology. But I was a young man in a great hurry, unwilling to enter fresh indentures, and finding myself not needed on the confused site of Hatshepsut's temple at Der el-Bahri, I evaded the obligation by making work among such Greek things as are in Egypt. I had no great success, and it was the best result of my Egyptian years that two Oxford scholars, who searched with me for papyrus scraps in the Fayûm desert one winter, were encouraged thereafter by my patrons to embark on a course which has led them to European fame. Clinging still to my old love Asia, I diverted my interest from Nile to Euphrates by making between seasons a journey which I have related in my *Wandering Scholar*; and, sure at last that my heart would never be in Egyptian work, I broke with my patrons after three years.

If, however, I had done little for them, I had done much for myself. In those three seasons, largely through becoming known to Petrie, and living with men who had served apprenticeship to him, I had learned to dig. When I set foot first in Egypt, I had no method in such search, nor any understanding that the common labourer's eyes and hands and purpose must be extensions of one's own. If an excavator, deaf to the first and greatest commandment of his calling, take no care to make his labourers better than unskilled navvies, what should he find except the things that a navvy could not miss in the dark? No strengthening of his European staff, no unwearied watching of native fools and knaves, will secure to the excavator the half of the precious things which lie in his soil. If the labourer, who is a fool, cannot see what is being turned over under his eyes, you at his side will see it no better, because you are not turning it over. The labourer who is a knave will see, but take good care you do not. Unless your men be seeking consciously and with intelligence in an interest which is theirs as well as yours, better leave the hiding places of ancient things alone. For every digger, who turns over a site without finding what is in it, destroys great part of what he should have found.

Moreover, in handling remains of imperishable antiquity in the Nile land, I learned to observe as an antiquary must. And some of his spirit was breathed into me; for when I went back to Egypt for a few weeks in 1897, I found myself regarding her ancient life more than her modern. But I was not to be won to Egyptian studies at the eleventh hour. Already designated Director, where I had been an unworthy student ten years before, I sailed for Athens, intending to take stock of the duties which were to be mine in the coming autumn, and to follow my proper trade by exploring a coast of Greek Asia. But temptation met me, and turned me out of the Antiquary's path.

CHAPTER I.

AN INTERLUDE.

I FOUND the representative of a great British journal in a difficulty. It was his hard task to gather news of several Balkan states, which one and all seemed determined to set about making history at the same moment. Crete was already ablaze; a Macedonian war was promised by Greece, and Bulgaria moved restlessly behind her frontier. Who knew what the others would hazard on flank and rear? I could speak fair Greek. Would I help him by undertaking Crete? It need not be for long. The Powers would soon make its peace, and deport the Greek soldiers who had just landed under the very guns of our ships. His actual correspondent, a Greek, was colouring his despatches to London white and blue. Would I replace him awhile? My temptation was brief. I had never been in Crete, and a scholar may rarely watch war.

I had not long to wait for it. As we drew to our anchorage inside the warships off Canea there were houses to be seen afire two miles inshore and rifles spitting up and down the slopes behind the town. The Turks had thought to revictual their threatened lines in peace during the hour of the Sunday office; but priests and people came out of church to fight. It was a small and desultory affair, from which less than a score of killed and wounded men were borne back at evening to the gates—patient Anatolian peasants for the most part, who had long served out their due time and fought without heat or reasoning why. Along with them came the corpses of two or three *bashibazuk* Cretans, Greek in feature and Greek in speech, Moslems by chance and all but ignorant of the faith which they had died to uphold. They were the first men slain in anger that I had seen.

I was to know Canea well in coming years; but that morning it looked very strange, with its mediaeval ways darkly shuttered and patrolled by smart marines of half a dozen nations and by slouching, thick-set Turks. The day might have been the morrow of a sack, so silent and desolate were the shops and houses about the quays, and so ruinous the inner streets. The great incendiary fires in the Christian quarter had been subdued only a day or two before, and the oil vats in the basements still smoked and stank. To this day, when I smell burning oil, I see Canea as I saw it first. As we ran up the harbour, the blackened shell of the Ottoman *Konak* on the heights to the left prepared us for what we were to see in the town. Our bluejackets and marines, we were told, had saved a part of the block, less with than despite the help of the frenzied Turks, among whom a certain grey-bearded Pasha had showed such erratic energy with a leaky hose, that it became necessary for our drenched marines to stay his zeal. Their commander called up his most respectable sergeant, and, pointing out the old gentleman as a person of consequence, bade his man wait a chance to withdraw the hose without offence. The sergeant saluted, wheeled, marched straight on the offender, and tapping him on the shoulder, remarked, with a genial but unprintable term of endearment and an even less printable counsel, that none of his sort was wanted there, and left him agape with empty dripping hands.

Canea was no pleasant abode at that moment. All inns, cookshops and coffee-houses, except the meanest, were burned or barred, and no cook or body-servant was for hire. The consuls, smoked out of Halépa a few days before, had broken into a deserted inn on the quayside, where their wives were setting before them such victuals as could be begged from the fleet. The journalists, who landed from every passing boat, lodged where and how men might in a ravished town, and a famous limner of battles kept life in him for the first few days with little but cauliflowers, oranges, and Greek brandy. Mine was a better fate. An old acquaintance of Cyprus days was commanding the Albanian police, and I found lodgment with him in the only tenanted house outside the walls, except one. In this last Chermside was living, who, like my host, sustained the British name for cool courage and quiet discharge of duty in those unquiet weeks. He showed me the lie of the land, talking of things Turkish as few men may talk, and franked me through the inner lines, where we found shoeless gunners with rags bound on feet and legs, stedfastly serving antique field-pieces with the slouch of woodmen who handle ox-carts on Anatolian hills.

The outposts lay fiercely beleaguered on a ridge further south, under the Sphakian summits—that dazzling background to the Venetian quadrilateral of Canea, which one sees from the sea like an embastioned city in a mediaeval illumination. Hapless outposts! They were the cause of all the bickerings between admirals and insurgents which it was to be my lot for three weeks to record. The Turks, too few to hold the outer lines in force, were not suffered by the Admirals to withdraw their pickets, lest the rebels, once on the crests, should shell the ships and the town. Yet no admiral would land his own men to support the defence and so lessen his fighting strength in the face of a faithful ally anchored alongside. So together and singly the leaders of the Powers held endless converse with bearded giants in broidered coats, and black-hatted men in sponge-bag suitings, who dubbed themselves captains and chiefs, and answered in halting French for the respect of the line; and Admirals vowed, in even less intelligible French, to shoot if the promises were broken. And broken they ever were, and once and again the Admirals shot, and Attic journals with inflammatory headlines, "Anti-Navarino," or "England massacres Christendom," egged on mobs to hoot the nameboard on the Grande Bretagne Hotel, and demand that the sanctuary of Hellenism on the Acropolis be closed for ever to the Barbarians of the West. Nor was Athens less than right according to her lights. True enough, it was we who led the shooting, and we who did almost all the blockading in Crete, for no other reason than that our gunners could shoot the best and our coal bunkers were kept full, and our crews did not mutiny for shore-leave where it could not be granted, and we alone had on the spot many war-craft of light draught and high speed.

But those bombardments ought never to have been necessary. With a few European bluejackets on guard

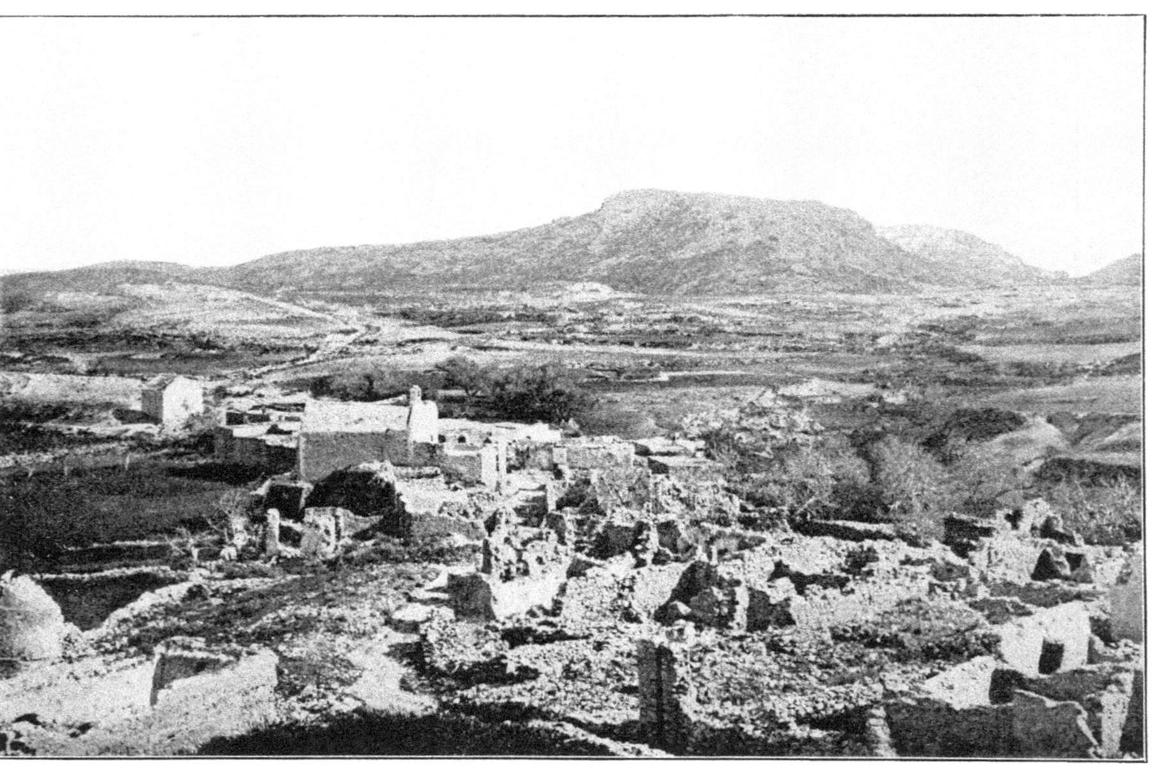

A WRECKED MOSLEM VILLAGE OF CRETE.

Facing p. 25.

at each blockhouse, the lines would never have been molested at all. The Admirals should have known Greeks better than to trust them on such vicarious parole as was given by caps and black hats, whether on the heads of chiefs or no. No Greek may answer surely for any other Greek, since individualism and intolerance of discipline are in the blood of the race. In the stormy history of Levantine religious warfare you may note one unvaried law of consequence. Where the Moslem has prevailed, the votaries of the two creeds have resumed peaceful life as of old, the Christian knowing that Moslems act under orders as one man, and that when Islam is triumphant its Gibeonites are secure of their lives. But if Christians gain their freedom, the Moslem leaves the land of his birth. For whatever pledges the new authorities may give, he knows for his part that, since Eastern Christianity supplies no social discipline, each Christian will act on occasion as seems best in his own eyes.

I had been in Canea three days when trouble arose in the town itself. Bairam was near, and the hundred and a half armed Albanian policemen, who were commanded for the nonce by my messmate and an Arnaut colonel, had been begging during some days, as their yearly custom was, an instalment of ready money for the feast. But the Turkish Treasury was empty, and the Powers supplied no funds. Put off, therefore, with vague answers to a demand which was no worse than fair, seeing they had touched no pay for months, some of the Albanians left their duty, and, rifles in hand, beset their commander with ever louder clamour for arrears. It is no British way to yield to threats. Weapons, they were told, must first be laid down, and then that should be done which could be. But Albanians part hardly with their arms, and these had often been deceived. Force must be used.

With another journalist I was warned privily that at a certain hour the Albanians would be surrounded in their barrack by European marines, who, however, were not to shoot. Should the Albanians still refuse to be disarmed, they would be charged with the bayonet. So to the barracks a little before the appointed time we two went, and posted ourselves on the stairway at the end of the large entrance hall behind the squatting Albanians, who watched curiously one squad of marines after another deploy into the courtyard, as for some review. Presently all was ready. The officers appeared from the guardroom, and once more bade the Albanians give up their arms. The men jumped to their feet, and a voice shouted in Turkish, *Verma!*—"Give not!" A squad of marines with fixed bayonets advanced to the door—nervous Italians, to whom the seniority of their Admiral secured pride of place. Two or three Albanians fired at sight, and hit an Italian with two balls. Instantly, its orders to charge forgotten, the whole Italian squad blazed point blank into the hall. We were standing two or three steps above the mass of the mutineers, and the rifles threw high. I was conscious all in a moment of jets of puffed flame, of shimmering blue blades, of a bullet humming by my ear, of a long scar ripped suddenly in the wall plaster at my side, of a big Albanian writhing at the stairfoot; and then we two non-combatants were skipping up the steps, taking three at a stride.

On the upper floor, where the temporary offices of government were, we found Armenian clerks frantically upsetting tables and bureaus, and thrusting them against doors. The rifles still barked below, and we thought for an instant of dropping from a window; but suddenly all firing ceased. Forcing a way back to the stairhead through a distracted crowd, which prayed us to say what was coming, we listened a moment, and then gingerly stepped down, I for one sore afraid of seeming afraid. In the hall all was very still. The cowed Albanians were flattening themselves against the walls, as though they would pass through the solid stones; a sound of groaning came from a barrack-room on the left, and two figures lay motionless in the middle of the floor. The Italians still fidgetted outside, with rifles levelled through windows and doorways, ready to fire. I walked out as slowly as I thought decent, and turning the flank of the Italian squad, went across to our own Marines, who were in fighting formation, the front rank on the knee. "Better out o' that, old man," called out a private. "What's their bag?" said a boy with a sword. I told him as well as I knew. "Pretty poor!" he grumbled. "Those fellows can't shoot for nuts!"

The leading squad got the word, entered at the charge, and met no resistance. I followed, and found that the loyal Albanian colonel had been shot twice, and, it was said, by his own men. He held out only a few minutes more. The Albanians' arms were passed outside; the mutineers, if mutineers they should be called, were marshalled into one room, and, as all seemed over except the caring for the wounded, the laying out of dead, and the arresting of ringleaders, I went off to the telegraph office, meeting belated and raging colleagues at every few yards, and wrote a despatch for London with not too firm a hand.

A wrangle ensued over the disposal of the prisoners. My messmate, who held his temporary commission from the Sultan, stood out long for a word from Constantinople before he would hand them over to the Powers; but the Admirals overruled him. I went to see the men tied up and marched to the boats. Some of them, who knew me by sight as one who understood a little of their speech, appealed to me, asking what their crime had been. Indeed, I could not exactly say. They had asked, after their customary manner, for the bread due to them, and been given lead. I liked the business little, and I knew my messmate, who held by his men as they held by him, liked it less. He had stipulated there should be no shooting by the marines (nor would there have been had the leading squad been men of our own corps), and the death of a friend, the Albanian colonel, lay heavy on his soul.

The Turkish soldiery and the *bashibazuk* Cretans were reported enraged by the killing of the Sultan's men, and a vendetta was feared from the Albanian remnant. My messmate thought it better to stay at his post in the town, and I had to pass the night of the mutiny without him in the lonely house without the walls. A howling storm dashed rain on the windows. The Greek cook, forecasting a dismal fate for himself and all his kind on the morrow, lifted up his voice and wept. I lay in my clothes, listening for shots, and hearing them now and then, probably in the hills. Once and again I braved the rain and looked out from the roof to the dark town, and the wheeling beams of searchlights darting from Suda Bay to the crests of the hills; and the dismal dawn came none too soon.

Little else would break the monotony of life in Canea.

The rescue of the beleagured Moslems of Kandanos by a landing party of all tongues had been worth seeing, if one could have got there. But the ships slipped away round the island by night, leaving journalists in the lurch and nothing in the harbour that steamed, except a little Greek tug. We all bargained for her ; but one rose in the night, while his colleagues slept, and embarked on her alone. Savage was the joy on the quay when some hours later she was espied steaming back, having failed to make headway against a south-west gale, and succeeded in making her passenger sorely sick. Only one consul saw the affair. Like all the rest Biliotti was given at dead of night two hours' warning of the sailing of the ships. His colleagues went sleepily to the telegraph office and blocked the wires with demands for instruction from ambassadors, who were snug abed in Pera ; but Biliotti, asking no man's leave, stepped into his consular boat, and had the conduct of all negotiations at Kandanos. The action was of a piece with everything he did. No more fearless or self-reliant servant of Britain has ever lived than this son of the Levant, who has no drop of British blood in his veins.

For the rest the daily round was full of rather common tasks—of eternal *quid nunc?* of lobbying, of begging crumbs from official tables. The fame of the great newspaper which I served gained me the best consideration that consuls and commanders afloat and ashore will show to a journalist, and I was also so fortunate as to be known privately to more than one of those in power. But they grew almost as weary of my constant calls as I, and if they were often irritable and always reticent, who can blame them ? Least of all would I blame the commanders at sea, who had to rock at anchor month in and month out, with nothing to do ashore, and crews cramped, confined, and murmuring for lack of leave. The Cretan Moslems were too jealous of their women for bluejackets to be let loose, and more than one French crew went to the verge of mutiny. Later on, when Latin troops came to be quartered in Canea, things reached such a pass that it was thought well to send oversea for a bunch of less forbidden fruit. It came in charge of a portly dame. But the Turk, who was still in nominal command of the port, refused in the name of Islam to admit these earthy houris; and the Great Christian Powers, by their representatives assembled, invoked the Concert of Europe to secure the landing of four Levantine light o' loves.

My fellow-journalists were for the most part a genial crew, which looked on the wine when it was red, or indeed of any other hue, and took life as it came. A few were tiros like myself; the others had seen many campaigns and much of the habitable world, where they had learned a little of most men and tongues by the way. But I found that almost all had tried other callings, and taken at the last to their actual trade, less in love of it than in disgust of all others. Our common talk was of warriors and war, when it was not of our despatches and their effect on the civilised world. In this company one was taken at the value one set upon oneself, and all was held fair that might serve the interest of a master at the other end of a wire.

When all the Moslems were collected under the guns of the ships, and the Christians held willy nilly to truce, there was less than ever for us all to do. The eyes of Europe had already turned from Crete to Thessaly, and before March was half spent almost all my colleagues were gone to Greece. I followed them late in the month, and, halting at Athens again, was over-persuaded to resume my service on the Greek frontier. But it could not be for long. I had laid plans with a fellow antiquary to go to Lycia, and the fair season for a southerly coast would soon be on the wane.

I took to myself, therefore, a helper, whom I had met at Athens eager for the front, and we went up together to Thessaly with all speed. At Volo we found good cheer and great clamour for war, and in every open space Reservists marshalled, who, if ever they had known soldier craft, had forgotten it. At Velestino, too, all was fair, and men gathered thick about us with cheers for England, who, as report said, had just checkmated a German plan to block Piraeus. But before we sighted the minarets of Lárissa (it is the one Greek town whose mean outline is still ennobled by their slender dignity), a northerly gale swept down, and rain began. Chilled to the bone and spattered with filth of unpaved streets, we came to the only hotel to find no lying room, even in a passage way. Our servant went out to seek some decent lodging, but in vain; and just at dark we took refuge in a wretched peasants' inn, where two soldiers were bribed to set free a single room for the three of us. Bugs were making their laboured but hopeful way over the floor towards the beds, and, lifting the coverlets, we found myriads already gathered in clusters on the mattresses. But if they waited there, they were cheated: for we spread sheets of rubber, knowing their distaste of its smell, and veiling our faces and hands, lay on the floor in our clothes. In the morning a Larissean, fearful who might be billeted on him, was glad to offer us a house far from soldiers' quarters, and we made ourselves comfortable enough in two empty but wholesome rooms.

There were some sixteen thousand soldiers in Larissa at that time, and during a fortnight I saw no man drunk and no common woman ply for hire. It was the Greek warrior's simple joy to stroll the streets, his little finger locked in a comrade's, and to sing in not unmusical harmony. Yet if he was a peaceable soldier, he was a lawless one. Once I heard a colonel reprove a strolling group which would have passed him without any gesture of salute. "Who are we that we are bidden to do such things?" said one, as the group moved on. When a battalion was being inspected before marching to the front, I watched man after man break rank to chat at ease with the bystanders, while the general was passing down the lines, and heard them laugh at his reproof. *Peitharcheia*, discipline,—what is that to a free-born Greek, whose birthright is to think for himself, and for you? It is said that the officer who, some weeks later, was ordered to blow up the Peneius bridge behind the retreating army exclaimed, "Am I a Vandal?" and the Turks found the bridge unhurt.

All here cried, "To Constantinople!" and mingled mutiny with their prayers. The King, they said, would not declare war because his Russian Queen had been forbidden by the Tsar. But if he would not, the voluntaries would. All southern Macedonia was waiting a sign to fall on the Turks, and in the space of a night the way would be clear to Salonica and beyond. If we went up to the outposts we should see in what heart were the Greeks and in what fear the Turks.

So on the second day we set out for the Malúna pass

above Elassóna. At Tírnovo the carriage seemed already to have passed out of Greece, so Turkish looked the little town with its shaded bazar and mosques and baths. At Ligária, where some two hundred kilted men were dancing before their tents in the morning sun and chanting war-songs, we were set on Hungarian cavalry horses, and escorted up the pass, with Olympus swelling grandly on the right. Two blockhouses and two batteries faced each other on the summit, and far below lay Turkish Elassóna, a dark patch within a white ring of tents. The officers (one red bearded, unlike a Greek), who had been watching this ring grow wider day by day, held more sober talk than we had heard in Larissa. "They are many more than we," said they, "and our beginning will perhaps be hard." "But," added the younger of the two, who was sweeping the Haliacmon valley with his glass, "all there wait to join us, and the end will be easy."

I asked safe conduct to the Turkish blockhouse, and was passed over the line. Two colleagues, or rivals, of whom we had heard nothing since their better-horsed carriage had overtaken us before Tírnovo, proved to be already seated in the little room, and plying the Albanian major with questions through a Greek interpreter. The latest come is ever most honoured by Turkish courtesy, and at sight of me the major made room on the divan at his side. I seated myself, and greeted him in my sorry Turkish. Overjoyed to be done with the Greek, the Albanian lapsed into his proper military speech, and sent for coffee. But the others took it ill, growled that we were now too many, swung out of the hut, and, when my visit was over, took me to task for having come between them and their news. Meanwhile the major had fenced with my inquiries about the Elassóna troops, and I had parried his about the muzzling of Moslems in Crete, and we parted as good friends as we had met, and about as wise. The officers of the kilted men at Ligária invited us to their midday meal, where was not overmuch to eat, but plenty of rough wine and the cheerful company of some French journalists, halting on their way to the crest. King George's health was drunk "if he allows us to make war," and then that of "all Powers who love Greece." Great Britain was the favourite of the hour, and the proposer of the toast breathed a fervent hope that "English guns were hungering for Russian meat." As a Briton who spoke Greek I was put up to reply, and I trust I bore the French love of Russia in mind; but I cannot say now what exactly may have passed, and have only a confused memory of driving away amid cheers, and becoming very drowsy on the Larissa road.

It remained to see how the case stood at the western end of the Cambunian lines; and on the following day we were trundling over the road to Tríkkala, with blockhouses, now Greek, now Turkish, always in sight on the crests to north. Except for a tedious ferry over Peneius and a noontide halt at the khan of Zarkos, near the scene of the only stout stand the Greeks would make on the frontier in the weeks to come, there was nothing to vary the monotony of a long drive between low hills and marshy plain. But the prospect of Pindus, one unbroken wall of snow, relieved the last hours. Trikkala, with its spacious square and imposing houses, promised better quarters than eventually we found in a tiny, dubious chamber, and we chose to pass much of our night in talking to one Greek officer or another. The five thousand men who were waiting here showed less rawness in their mien than the army of Larissa, and seemed better equipped for a coming war: but an officer anticipated all criticism by saying that Greece had no use for regulars. She was freed by guerilla fighters of the hills, and would conquer by the same. Forbearing to object that the campaign might take place chiefly in the open Thessalian plain, I asked an artilleryman if there were many of his service who could speak Turkish? "Not I, for one," he answered scornfully, "but our guns there can say what a Turk will understand." I hope they could, for probably they are in Turkey now.

From Kalabaka five kilted men were sent next day to escort us on a long march to the outposts above Diskáta. They were true soldiers of the hillman kind, lean, long-stepping, untiring, to whom the admirable Greek schools had given intelligence and interests little like those of our Highlanders. We talked, for example, as we strode together, about the Emperor Hadrian. The way lay under the Metéora rocks, and halting below the chief monastery, we summoned with loud shouts the "fishers of men." But their windlass remained still, and the kilted men, growing impatient, began to fire upwards. One or two bullets skimmed the prior's tiles, and a monk appeared at an opening to ask our pleasure. We called to him to let down the net, but pleading that his fellows were all at meat, he offered us no more than the cranky ladders of a perilous chain, which swayed in the wind against the overhanging cliff. We had neither stomach nor head for such escalade; but two of the soldiers dared it, and, once aloft, soon had the windlass manned and the net lowered. The rope had plainly seen many and better days, but up we must go. We lay down together in the meshes, which were gathered and hooked above; the rope strained, the net tightened, and we slowly rose, locked in an inextricable embrace, like a pair of bagged ferrets, spun, bumped the cliff, spun again for an eternity, till gaffed and drawn into the entry, we realised that we yet breathed.

The monks bade us coldly welcome, though we gave them time to finish meat while we looked at the dark church, whose only interest lies in its age, and climbed to the rounded summit of the rock, where fed eleven snow-white sheep and one coal-black, in memory, I suppose, of the apostolic Twelve. The keys of the Treasury were said to be with the Bishop elsewhere; but I suspect we might have been shown the precious things had it not been for the presence of our kilted guards, who treated the fathers with scant respect, and were evidently feared. The Prior bemoaned the coming war, complaining that no one would turn *kaloyer* now; he had but five monks all told. But the Bursar was a better patriot, who would breathe fire and slaughter, if the men of Athens did not make war. Where was Constantine tarrying who should lead the Greeks? Ah! who knew? he asked darkly.

The day was far spent when we saw the blockhouses at last, Greek to right, and Turk to left, on a low ridge. The way had lain through a wild and ill-tracked country, where were a few Vlach villages, of evil fame for past raiding and present brigandage; and from the frontier we looked north over a yet more savage prospect. Diskáta lay hidden by a shoulder of the hill, and nothing but a rough mule path came up from it. There were no such proofs of

Turkish assembly visible from this point, as we had seen from Malúna, and the half dozen infantrymen who squatted on the Turkish side of the line were tatterdemalions. The Haliacmon basin lay in deep purple shadow, and beyond it a tumbled sea of mountain waves, swelling to west and north, broke here and there in snows: on the other hand the bastions of Pindus rose against the sunset out of a blue-grey mist, which hid their roots and all the plain. But such beauties had lost any charm they may ever have had for our hosts, the two Greek officers in charge of the blockhouse. It was very lonely, they said, and how long would they be left there? One who had been on the hills fourteen months showed himself a more doubtful prophet even than the men of Malúna Would Macedonia indeed rise? If not, could the thin Greek line hold the Malakás pass, and how should he alone stem the unknown flood which might well up from Diskáta? Small blame to him for his doubts, with that five hour march over rough paths and unbridged streams to his nearest support!

The two were as lavish of good cheer as glad of our coming, and one kept the caraffe of *raki* replenished and the wine flowing free, while the other took his turn to patrol. After which surfeit, fevered already by our long tramp, we had broken sleep in a clean, cold soldier's room, and were up and about in good time to watch the first blush of day on the Pindus snows, and begin the tramp to Kalabáka again. We went back to Larissa by railway, and at the junction of Velestino I spied, to my surprise, a banker of my former acquaintance in Alexandria. I asked him what he did in this far province? "Business," he said, "in Kalabáka—some men to see there." The men, though I knew it not, were those voluntaries who would raid over the frontier some weeks later and compel war; and it was this banker, as kindly and brave a man as I have known, who financed that fatal venture of fanatic Hellenism. The following evils broke his heart, it was said, and he died not many months later.

In Larissa once more I had news both of the purpose of the Powers to prevent war, and of the exceeding unwillingness of the Greek court to yield to the desire of the mob. Prince Constantine was to come in a few days, but I was warned his mission was to hinder, not hasten outbreak. I resolved to await at least his coming, and busied myself with one more visit to the outposts, this time at the eastern end, by Rapsáni near Tempe; but we got little thereby except a sight of the Vale, and a deeper sense of the unfitness of the trailing conscripts met upon the road. It was strange to see Thessalian Turks peaceably tilling their fields, as the soldiers passed; and, maybe, they looked for war as little as I. The Prince came at last, to be met with salvoes of artillery and a solemn assurance "in the name of the Church of Larissa and the great martyrs of Crete" that all the hope of Greece was in him; but when he paraded the garrison, it was said he liked it ill. In any event weeks must yet pass before war would be declared (if ever), and my time was up. I yielded my place to my companion, and shipped at Volo with a heady pack of Greek patriots, each of whom, finding at dinner a Briton who understood his speech, exhorted the rest to be calm, and forthwith fell into frenzy. Let all Europe come on! Greece in her turn would blockade Europe. "Ah! what you really fear is Hellenism, the Great Power to be! England covets Crete—that is the secret cause of all!" I had heard more than enough by coffee time, and sought peace on deck watching the hills darken behind Thermopylae, where once upon a time Greeks died in silence.

I was to play the journalist once more about a month later, when returned from Lycia to find the war begun and, indeed, all but over. Faithful news was wanted from Crete concerning both the plans of the rebels in that day of Greek despair and the state of the Moslem islanders, now almost all gathered into Candia within a fence of British and Italian tents. I was bound for home, but agreed to take Crete on the way; and landing at Canea, I was allowed to go out to the rebel outposts on Akrotíri, with an Italian bugler and a stalwart Highlander of our Seaforths, whose native brae was Wapping. The rebels swarmed out of their shelters at the bugle's note, and, after brief parley, let me pass in. Except for black Cretan kerchiefs bound about their heads, they were all in serge clothing of sailor fashion, got I know not how or whence, and all had Belgian arms. They led me to a shady spot, set chairs, and began to talk in Greek. But presently the chief, a man of consequence who had been in the Island Council under the Pact of Halépa, came up in haste, and finding all speaking at once, proposed French. Thus question and answer passed in quiet, and babel arose only when my words were summarised in the common speech from time to time with more rhetoric than I had used. The sum of an hour's converse was this. The rebels were more set than ever on rebellion. If one army of the Greeks had run, another would stand, and the fleet was undefeated still. Had the

Cretans ships, they would send fifteen thousand men to defend their Mother; for how could they desert her in her sorrow? They did not wish to stand alone in insular freedom, for there was none in Crete fit to govern, and they feared treachery of one to another. If the Powers occupied the island, the British would fall out presently with the Russians and call the Turks back. "Vassos and his Greeks may stay or go—we care not. We shall fight on. We have food enough here, though little corn, but in the western parts there is some dearth. Still the blockade can be cheated. What have we to lose now by holding out or to gain by giving in? Most of us have lost long ago all we had. The Moslem Cretans must leave the island, for their hate is too fierce for peace." It came to this—they defied us, well knowing that no one Power would be suffered by the rest to land enough men to sweep their hills: and I rose convinced that union with the Hellenic kingdom is the inborn hope of a Cretan. He sucks it in with his mother's milk, and breathes it at her knee; reason is powerless against his sentiment, and to use it worse than vain. We parted in peace, and my Wapping Scot, though apparently he had kept his eyes front all the hour with the wooden rigour of a snuff-seller's ensign, remarked on every detail of each rebel's dress and arms as we trudged back over the rocks.

I went on to Candia, and could find no clean lodging. The Christian houses were shut and barred, and, as the whole town was unquiet and every native Moslem a *bashibazuk* armed to his teeth, it seemed wise to live near the harbour. I applied to our vice-consul, a Cretan Greek, who was to perish in the massacre of the following year. He had a house, he replied, of his own, hard by the quay, and very clean. It was let to a Corfiote, who was not very well; but he and his wife kept to one room, and doubtless would gladly hire me the others. I asked nothing better, and went off to view. The house seemed both clean and convenient and I passed from room to room, till I reached a closed door in the upper storey. A woman, who answered my knock, said her husband would be glad to arrange the matter. He was in bed, and not very well; but would I be pleased to enter and talk to him? I stepped in, and sat some minutes by his bed-head in the close air. He looked wasted, and at last I asked if it were fever of the country he had? "No," said he. "Smallpox. This is the twelfth day." I fled, and expecting the deadly rash to break out any day, found another house, wherein I tried to make shift. But the windows looked on the Cathedral yard, in which an Italian regiment of very young soldiers bivouacked each night, drinking, singing, and fighting from dusk to dawn: and in the end I pitched a tent on the ramparts, near the camp of a Mountain Battery of ours. The days were spent in watching the route-marching of our troops, listening to all that commandants would tell me, and riding out towards the rebel lines. On these excursions I visited Cnossus for the first time, and dreamed of digging in the Palace of Minos, some of whose lettered stones already stood revealed. Indeed I was offered a squad of sappers, who might begin the search there and then; but I refused it for lack of time and in distrust of soldier diggers, whom I had known in Alexandria for the best navvies but the worst finders of antiques in the world. The lesser Bairam, the feast of Abraham's sacrifice, was at hand, and I waited only for it. If ever the town was to rise and hurl itself on the exultant cordon of rebels, it would be then. But in the end the feast passed without any worse incident than the firing of many bullets from the town over our camp, perhaps at hazard, but, perhaps, also in our despite ; and by the middle of May I could bid farewell for ever, as I thought, to the island of Crete.

CHAPTER II.

LYCIA.

THE war, for which I had waited in vain, broke out when I was far from its alarms. It had long been arranged that I should report on ancient sites in Lycia, for whose excavation certain scholars, jealous for the fame of Fellows, proposed to found a fund. Three cities offered the best hope of success, Xanthus, Pátara, and Myra, and to survey these I left Athens with one companion as soon as I was free of Thessaly. We reembarked at Smyrna on a Greek coaster, hoping to find a small sailing vessel for hire in the first Lycian port of call; but deceived in this, we had to keep on with the Greek, and try our luck in the busier harbour of Castellórizo.

Of all the Greek isles Castellórizo lies most apart, outside the Archipelago, and nearly a hundred miles east of Rhodes, its motherland. The main coast over against it is the wildest of Anatolia, piled ridge on ridge from surf to snow-line, and inhabited by few except wandering shepherds. Descendants of sturdy Rhodians, who would not abide under the Hospitallers, hold the barren rock, and live by exploiting the sea. The Turk is overlord; but we found his representatives, a *mudir* and half dozen excisemen, who were dependent on Greek keels for all their communication with the mainland, chastened in demeanour and quick to defer to quayside opinion. This set strongly in our favour; and forbearing to demand our papers, they offered weak propitiatory coffee, and withdrew to inactivity. Heavily sparred brigs and two-masted caiques were packed that morning so close into the basin that a man might cross it dryshod; but the magazines and counting-houses round the port bore witness that these ships plied a gentler trade than that which once made a Castellóriziote sail a terror in the Levant. In fact, they traffic between the smaller Anatolian ports and Alexandria, where you may often see their antique high-pooped hulls lying under the Breakwater, and what they carry is chiefly firewood and charcoal, cut and burned on the Lycian hills. "The mainland, then, is yours?" we asked. "Ours, as much as anyone's," replied sons of corsairs. "We take what we want. Whom should we pay?"

Just ten years before I had had a passing vision of the isle from the deck of a rusty tramp steamer, which called in vain for freight, and sheered off again ere I was well awake; and one thing especially I had not forgotten, the beauty of the fisher-folk whom we had passed drifting on a windless bay under the sunrise, "dark faces pale against a rosy flame." The type in Castellórizo is the finest among latter-day Hellenes. There you will find Praxitelean heads in the flesh—find the oval face, with brows spread broad and low beneath clustering hazel hair. Grey-brown almond eyes lie wide, deep, long and liquid; noses stand forth straight and faultless; upper lips and chins are short, and mouths mobile and fine. But the straight fall of the skull behind should warn you that the race is old, if a certain meagreness of tissue and over-refinement of feature have not already betrayed its age. Women, who had three-year babes at their knees, showed too much bone, and little softness of outline in their faces; but none the less we thought them very beautiful, gazing about us with as little discretion as may be used in an Eastern society, and marvelling that painters and sculptors had not happened on this dream of fair women. The men, when they had shown us their pretentious marble church, garish with gilt carvings and Russian icons, led on to the schools, and first to that of the girls. It should have been holiday; but I suspect the classes were warned as soon as we were seen to land, for no Greek can deny himself the pleasure of showing his scholars to a western stranger. As we came within the door the serried ranks arose, and the eyes of fifty maidens, each fit to bear Athena's *peplus*, looked into our own. Miserably we heard a hymn, miserably stammered incoherent thanks, and miserably fled. Who were we that we should patronise a choir of goddesses?

The town, more regularly laid out than most of its kind, rises in a horseshoe, tier on tier, from the port, whence radiate steep stone ladders dividing the wedges of habitation, as in the *cavea* of an ancient theatre. We strolled from one horn of the bay to the other, admiring such nice cleanliness of streets and houses as you may see in the richer Cyclad isles, in Santorin, for example, and here and there on the Turkish coast, but seldom or never on the Greek mainland. In Castellórizo to be dirty is to confess social failure. The housewife of the most speckless floor holds her head highest, and her husband's prodigality in whitewash and paint would delight a London landlord. Blue balconies overhanging the roadway, and shutters and doors of startling hue seemed fewer than in other Greek towns of like pretension; and glimpses of interiors assured us that more than the outside is here made clean. The windows look for the most part not on the street, but on high-walled courts, in the secretive Moslem manner, having been set thus perhaps in darker days, when the island was still a pirate's nest. But many a heavy street door was thrown wide that morning to reveal the garden-fringes of orange and lemon and almond trees which framed geometric patterns of many-coloured pebbles; and we had to parry laughing invitations from women-folk, standing in holiday velvet and lace by their entrance-ways.

At length we climbed out on to the saddle of the twin-peaked rock, which is all the island. The southward slopes looked too naked for even a goat's subsistence, and our self-appointed guides said they had but one precious spring of running water. To northward the Lycian seaboard, rising to points and bars of snow, filled the distance. In the nearer view lay the burnished strait of Antiphellus, with a fishing fleet becalmed, and at our feet the white crescent of the town. Pointing to the mainland, we asked what concern the islanders had there? They pastured their few flocks, was the reply, cut wood, burned charcoal, and owned orange and olive gardens or small farms. There were, indeed, several little colonies of Castellóriziote squatters, and one large village of their folk, Dembré, on the coast eastwards; but no one went there "since the measuring." The last words were said quickly and low, and when we sought an interpretation of them, each man looked at his neighbour, as the habit is on Ottoman soil when talk has chanced on some public sore. Even we might be spies. We asked no more, knowing we should learn presently whatever was to be learned; for Dembré lies near ancient Myra, whither we were bound.

We found a fishing boat waiting approval at the quay, and the bargain was soon struck. One-eyed Antóni, his son, and his nephew bound themselves to do our pleasure for ten days at least, if they might bring back a load of Fíneka oranges, should they chance to meet with it. It sounded a pleasant cargo, and we agreed. In the early afternoon we pushed off, the light breeze being reported fair; but in the open the deceitful airs died away, and we fell to rocking on a sullen oily swell, which was rolling up from south-west to hurl itself on the iron coast, with a distant murmur of surf. There was nothing to do for hours but to follow the shadow of the sail. Our Greek cook (the same who had shared my vigil on the night of the mutiny at Canea) dived under the half-deck, and was presently very sick. He had been engaged on his word that he had served the Messageries Maritimes of France; but he now explained between paroxysms that his service had been done in an engineer's house ashore. I doubt if even so much was true, for later on I was to hear him through the thin wall of a hut brag to gaping peasants that he was the bastard of a French general, and had known me from my childhood! The one thing sure in his past was that he had sung in cafés on the Galata quay, and the one thing certain in his future that, except in the near neighbourhood of quays, he would prove useless throughout thc cruise.

In the waning day the sails filled, and the boat began to slip fast and faster eastward before a whistling breeze, which had caught up the swell. Cliffs loomed near, and in the last of the light a surf-washed wall sheered up right ahead. Antóni smiled at my doubts, and held on his course till it seemed we must crash ashore. Then the rock parted this way and that: we twisted to left, to right, and to left again, and lo! a great water and the long unruffled track of the moon on the land-locked bosom of Kékova. We ran to a berth under a shaggy hillock crowned with dim fantastic outlines of Lycian rock-tombs—the forgotten cemetery of Aperlae—and spying a single light ashore, landed to try the house for supplies. The Greek fishermen who inhabited it, Castellóriziote colonists known to Antóni, sold us eggs and a fowl; but they were strangely disturbed at sight of us, and dumbfoundered when told we were bound for Dembré. I bethought me they might be smugglers on occasion, and asked no questions, but feeling that something was not well with Dembré, planned to avoid the village on the morrow by running to the mouth of the Myra river and walking thence to the ruins. But next morning the south-wester, which sped us merrily on an even keel down the Kékova strait, was beating up so rough a sea in the open that Antóni would not risk the longer run, and beaching us on the nearest sand, sent his boat back to shelter.

We had to make our way, therefore, towards the village by an unfrequented path through the gardens, and we met no man. The streets were very silent, and reaching a coffee-house we turned into it to seek a guide. A group of Greeks stared at us open-mouthed,

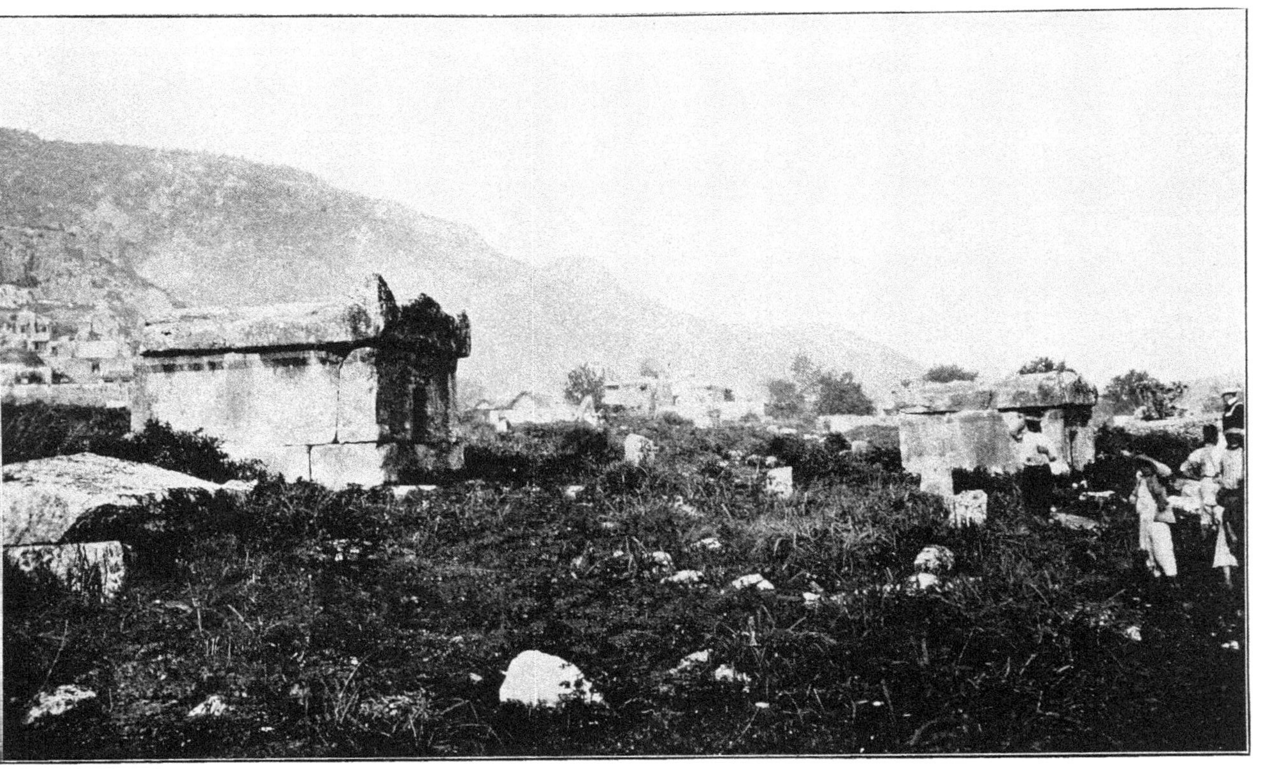

LYCIAN TOMBS.

Facing p. 48.

THE THEATRE OF MYRA.

Facing p. 49.

and scarcely replying to our salutations, slunk one by one away; nor was the obsequious host less perturbed. In less than a minute a heavy footfall sounded without, and first one police-trooper and then another strode in. Who were we? We told our nationality. Had we papers? Yes, and in order for the coast so far as Adalia. What might be our business here? To see the ruins of Myra. How had we come? By boat, we said. Where was that boat? It had run to Kékova. Then back you go to it at once, said they. I replied that we were come to see Myra, would certainly see it, and must, moreover, sleep the night here, for it would be too long a tramp back to the boat, which was lying we knew not exactly where. *Olmáz! Yasák!* they said in one breath. Impossible! It is forbidden! Where, then, was their superior officer? Up country, they answered. Well, I said, rising, you will send our papers up to him, and meanwhile we walk on to Myra. And so we did, none hindering us, but none agreeing to guide; and unmobbed for once, we roamed about the vaults and horseshoe of the great Theatre, and climbed unwatched the rock-cut stairway which leads to the great carved cliff of tombs. Thus some hours passed pleasantly before we saw a trooper and an unmounted man coming across the fields. The trooper brought word that since we were here and said we would not go away, we might stay the night, and his companion, a Greek, would house us. Whereafter both settled down to stay beside us; but the trooper, tired by his gallop inland, soon fell asleep in the shade, and the Greek, following me out of earshot, unfolded at last the mystery of the Measuring of Myra.

Dembré, it appeared, has two titles to fame, over and above the fact that it once was Myra. It is the nearest considerable village to the great Kékova harbour, and it possesses, in the half-buried church of the martyr Nicholas, a shrine to which the Orthodox communities of the world pay no small reverence. Now, from time to time European warships find their way into the Kékova pool, and more than one has chanced to make some stay. Their visits have passed not unremarked by the Ottoman government. If Russia, or Austria, or England should seek a Levantine harbour, what better than Kékova? When Russia holds out the Gospel in front, Turks look for a sword at her back, and therefore uneasiness became panic when it was reported that a Russian consul had bought of a Greek farmer the shell of the church of Saint Nicholas and the land about it. It was said he was proceeding to excavate the shrine, to set it in order, and to arrange for the resumption of the holy office, and already was in treaty for the sites of two other churches which stand amid the ruins of Andráki, close to the eastern mouth of Kékova. The Porte resolved to act. A commission of three officials appeared in Dembré, proclaiming a mandate to "measure" the village, its houses and its lands, with a view to readjusting its contribution to the Imperial Exchequer; and measure they did with admirable deliberation, living the while at the charges of the farmers. Here be it observed that the Ottoman Law, as it was then, warned all men to leave buildings, lands, or other real estate untouched during such interval, usually short enough, as must elapse between the making of a survey and the final notification of assessment. Neither might any kind of property be bought or sold, nor could a barn, a house, a fence be built or even repaired. Two years ago the measurers had vanished from Dembré, and from that day to the hour of our arrival the village had heard no word of its assessment.

Imagine those years. The village was frozen as by a spell. A special police-post was established landwards, and all neighbours were searched as they approached or left the suspect community. The weekly market ceased, and all commerce of men whatsoever Houses gaped to wind and rain, but they might not be made good; and lands went out of cultivation for lack of seed. This state of things endured weeks, months, a year, till, sick with hope deferred, some householders, abandoning all they had, slipped away of dark nights aboard Castellóriziote caiques, and passed on to free Greek soil, fearful of being retrieved from their mother-isle. Round the remainder in Dembré the cordon was drawn closer; but a few others managed to flee as time went on, leaving their houses tenantless and their gardens to the riot of weeds. Outsiders, even kinsmen, shunned the banned village, and were shunned in turn, if bold enough to enter, lest suspicion attach of trafficking or plotting escape. No formal taxes were levied, but the police had to live, which came to the same thing, or to more, in the end; and currency grew rarer and rarer in the village, little or none coming from without. It was the survivors of a lately prosperous community that we had seen hanging about the streets, fearful to act or speak, watching for a release that never came. My informant supposed nothing could be done to help them. He himself would suffer, of course, as soon as we were gone, for his entertainment of us to-night, forced though it was. His plaint was uttered less in anger than with a certain air of apology, as a man, conscious of futility, might complain of the weather or any other act of God. The idea that the Common Law had been shamefully abused to his undoing, had probably never occurred to him, his view of Law being that of most poor folk, that it is wholly external, the voice of an irresponsible will to be endured or evaded like any other tyranny. And his Padishah had only acted as Kings have ever acted in the East, from the Great King, the King of Assyria, to the latest Sultan or Shah.

Afterwards we visited that fatal church. It is claimed for it (perhaps extravagantly) that it is the same in which the great Bishop of Myra, who is become the patron saint of fishermen, and inspires the Christmas dreams of children over half the world, ministered and was buried. St. Nicholas lies at Bari now; but the violated place of his first rest is shown at Dembré in a recess fenced from the northern aisle of the basilica by a low screen of varied marbles somewhat more recent in date than the saint's day. The apse retains the form of the original Tribunal, with the stone throne set in a semicircle of seats, moss-grown and stained with green slime; and taken for all in all, this church is the most interesting memorial of the early days of Christianity, in the land where Paul conducted the first Christian mission.

Our host entertained us as well as his poor means allowed, and spread long rugs on his low divans. In the morning light I was struck with the beauty of their hues, and asked their age, which seemed to be some seventy years. The owner whispered to my servant, Would I buy? He wished to sell all he had, gather a little privy

THE REPUTED TOMB OF ST. NICHOLAS AT MYRA.

Facing p. 52.

cash, and make his escape, and he asked no more than a fair price. He was willing to carry the load five or six rugged miles, and I have those rugs still. We found the boat in a sheltered cove of Kékova, and tacking down the strait, brought up under the shore of deserted Dóliché, where we fished and ate our catch under the moon, and cradled on the gentle swell, slept careless of cockroaches and fleas.

On the morrow Antóni set sail westward, but we made slow way, for the wind was contrary, and it was not till three days later that, after revisiting Castellórizo, we stood in to Kalamáki bay about the third hour. With difficulty horses were hired for the road to Pátara and Xanthus, and we stumbled out of the little *scala* early in the afternoon; but ill mounted on a rough road, we did not sight the vale of Pátara till the sun was low. Patches of stagnant water, catching the level rays, glistened here and there like gold foil on the poisonous greenness of the hollow; while other patches, grey in shadow and golden-brown in light, gradually resolved themselves into ruins standing in deep marsh. A tethered horse grazing on the rim of the slough, a faint tinkling of goat bells, and three black tents near a pine-log shelter alone betrayed the presence of man on the holiest site of Lycia.

Certain of swampy ground ahead, we dismounted; for most Anatolian horses, whether from heredity or from early experience of bogland, will fall into a paroxysm of terror at the sight of water in the path, and I have known the most battered pack-jade rear and prance like Job's war-horse rather than pass a gutter. So afoot we went down to see Pátara. These cumbered sites of dead cities may refresh the soul, but surely they vex the body. The curse of Lost Paradise seems to brood over them, bidding the longest thorns and the stoutest thistles grow and multiply between their stones. Snakes and scorpions wait for the unwary hand in every cranny, and all blocks seem to have fallen edge uppermost or to be ready to turn under a hasty foot.

The ruins of Pátara lie round its silted harbour, which is become a reedy morass. A fortress of the Byzantine age has been the last permanent habitation; and along the broken crenellations of its walls we followed clumsily the soft-shod feet of an agile Yuruk boy. It was no holiday ramble. The wall was a mere *arête* between inky depths to left and a slimy jungle to right; it was often broken and always unsafe, and over its rottenest parts passage had to be forced through clumps of rank vegetation. We made slow progress, marked by the splashing of loose stones into the pool and the scurrying of its myriad gruesome tenants, and when we had struggled to dry land, near the sand-choked ruin of the Theatre, it was high time to seek some lodging for the night.

Far up the marsh the cry of a goatherd driving his flock to higher ground sounded faintly amid a responsive jangle of gathering bells; and loud in our ears sang the first mosquitoes of sundown. What pests must rise from that rotting slough of a summer night, making a camp intolerable, even on the heights above! But in chill April weather one might hope to pass the dark hours well enough. We made for the pine-log shelter and the three black booths, and finding the first full of dung, wherein fleas and ticks unnumbered lay in wait, sent our Greek ahead to parley with the Yuruks.

THE SAND-CHOKED THEATRE OF PATARA.

Facing p. 54.

This was a tactical mistake. Hospitality, even in the East, is more often enforced by public opinion than offered out of the fulness of the heart. Therefore, you should meet your possible host half-way without the hesitancy which the polite code of the West prescribes: appeal boldly to his tribal conscience; identify yourself with his dwelling or his kin; touch his beard, his knees, his head, his salt, his tent-rope. All nomads are encased in tribal selfishness, and among the most exclusive are the Yuruks, who wander under the shadow of a government wholly external to them, that takes all it can and gives nothing in exchange. What do they want with the apparatus of official Ottoman civilisation, with police, only seen at the heels of the publican, with the local *mairie*, only entered at the heels of the police, with new roads and spidery bridges which their sagacious asses avoid? All these things they curse in one breath with the provinces of Yemen and Hasa, to which their sons are spirited as conscripts. Such men offer no spontaneous welcome to the casual stranger—a tax-gatherer as likely as not, or a spy of the local assessor—who knows?; and a party like ours, not strange enough in gait or guise to rouse that curiosity which overmasters suspicion, will fare ill if it waits an invitation.

The Greek came back to say we were among bad men, and had best go back to Kalamáki, night though it was. But we had no mind to remount our jaded beasts and stumble for four hours over that execrable path, and the Yuruks looked honest folk enough. So doing last what we should have done first, we walked straightway into the largest tent and sat down by the ashes of its hearth. No one showed surprise. We were within our social right by the code, and the owner had no choice but to follow and speak the customary words of welcome. But suspicion clouded his simple mind, and we had to go through that exasperating Ollendorfian dialogue, which, in one language or another, must be held on arrival wherever men have been taught by long experience to conceal their wealth.

"Have you barley for our beasts?"

"We have no barley."

"But we give money." (*Chins jerked and tongues clicked to imply incredulity and denial.*)

"Well—have you chopped straw?"

"There is none, Wallah!"

"Good—nor eggs?"

"*We* have no eggs." (*Abundance in the next camp.*)

"Nor milk?"

"To-day, none." (*Yesterday and to-morrow, never to-day.*)

"Nor butter, nor bread, nor anything?"

"Not anything, by the head of God!"

"But these fowls, they are barren?"

"Ai-i! they lay eggs, God be praised!"

"And those nanny-goats, they are all dry?"

"Wallah! They make milk."

"Then, by God's will, we stay. Quick! barley, milk, eggs! We stay."

And in nine cases out of ten your simple wants will be supplied; and although sooner or later you must parry the inevitable prayer for those rejuvenating philtres, of which all Franks are understood to hold the secret, you will part best of friends at dawn from unwilling hosts of the evening before.

Should an Eastern depart from his indifferent reserve

and greet you cordially at first sight, beware of him. He meditates some particular motive of self-interest. A few years ago certain official assessors of land-tax on their way up the left bank of the Nile suddenly found the obstruction, which had embittered their earlier progress, yield to a spirit of frank hospitality. Sheikhs and notables came forth to greet them. The best of the village was at their service, and the fullest revelation was made at once of the wealth of each community, and especially the high value of its lands. Meanwhile another Commission, advancing *pari passu* up the contrary bank, was equally surprised by a like change in the peasants' demeanour. Its business was to purchase ground for the track of a State Railway, and lo! field after field along the proposed line was hardly worth an old song. Thus for awhile were both Commissions in clover. Then weeping and wailing broke out behind them, and obstruction became more dogged than ever in front. The assessors had been mistaken for the railway surveyors, the surveyors for the assessors.

With us, however, all would now go well. Neither our clothes nor, truth to tell, our halting Turkish reminded the old Yuruk of any publican he had ever known. Pine-logs were heaped on the embers, tobacco-boxes offered and accepted, buttermilk and unleavened dampers brought in by the wrinkled dame. The patriarch, readily unbosoming his griefs after the manner of his kind, told how he had broken up and sowed a bit of Noman's land, and promptly found it assessed as a field under irrigation; how his last plough-ox had been taken to discharge a debt not half its value, and his son, the support of his age, was gone to the Yemen—never, God be witness, to return. Wallah! *he* knew the Government! The tale sounded pathetic to our ears, and we tried awkwardly to sympathise with the teller; but we got no help from our Greek, reassured by this time, and well aware how light such woes lie on the bird-like souls of wanderers who are here to-day, dispersed to-morrow, and fatalist above the settled folk. He chimed in with ribald pleasantries, reminiscent of his Gálata days, to the delight of the patriarch and his son, little used to urban wit.

His indecencies, but half understood, seemed no affair of mine, and thankful to be discharged from the talk, I ceased to listen. The night had fallen luminous, with a rising moon, and profoundly still. Not a needle stirred in the pine fronds. Only the flat note of a bell sounded now and again from the fold as a beast turned in his lair; and in the pauses of talk one might hear even the faint intermittent crepitation of stones, trees, and earth, respiring the heat of the past day. But whenever, to the relief of unaccustomed eyes, the smoky fire died down, a strident column of mosquitoes would sail in by the door to dispute our persons with the fleas.

Such tent-dwellers seem lighter of heart than the men of Turkish towns and villages, merrier perhaps for having less between them and the sky. There is this to be said for tent-life in a warm clime—it exhilarates, like the casting off of clothing; and perhaps for this reason civilised men of other climes have so much hankering for it, despite its insecurity and its plague of blowing dust, and the noonday heat and the cold in the dawn. But the canvas booth is not meant for house-dwellers who carry with them much furniture and many scattered possessions, and would sit high and stand upright. It should be low to cheat the wind, and empty of all that may gather dust—a mere canvas burrow, such a shelter from draught and sun and dew as suits the simplicity and the poverty of minds in which want of occupation and variety in life leaves no void to be filled by the morbid introspection dear to civilised solitaries.

The woman took no part in the discourse, nor did she share the meal with her husband after his guests were satisfied. But having tendered him the bowl with the gentlest motion of one palm towards her breast, in obedience to an immemorial instinct of reverence for the male, she sank on her heels to coax the fire and croon over the ashes, throwing now and again a question at us, till some pastoral duty called her outside the tent. It was perfect domestic accord. Man and woman without friction, question or strife, evidently sufficed together for all the necessary functions of existence. She, in her constant performance of physical labours, had probably never known the woes of either her toiling or her idle Western sisters: for her no sexual cravings unappeased, no assumption of the manly part, no fear of loneliness in middle life or age. If she must be obedient in all things, even to stripes, the inexorable opinion of a simple society would protect her from physical tyranny. For in the nomad's tent the rod is held a fool's weapon, and shame is on him who can rule his household with no other, or fails to pay in a multitude of punctilious ways due honour to his wife.

. . . .

I must have fallen into uneasy sleep, for, when roused by the cold, as much as by insect legions, I found the talk ceased and the talkers slumbering, feet to fire. A sea-wind, rising gustily, fanned an intermittent glow in the heart of the embers, and their dusky gleam revealed the old Yuruk a moment, lying supine, with his head on the lap of his dame, who sat stark asleep against the tent-pole. Seen thus, the two looked less like human beings than gnomes, or survivors of some primaeval race which worshipped other gods. And so, in a sense, they were. Though the Yuruks profess Islam, Allah has not the best of their private allegiance; and under his name they revere, without ritual or articulate creed, some private tribal god, with whom they feel the possibility of more intimate communion. The All-Father of the Arabs has no more chased the petty gods of place and tribe out of the Nearer East than He of the Hebrews. He has been accepted, indeed, as a strictly constitutional monarch, or rather, perhaps, as a Judge of Appeal who may resolve now and then those age-long feuds in which tribal gods involve their human kin; but, for the rest, accepted only in so far as he prescribes no duty but towards himself. He is an immaterial Allah, without parts or earthly semblance, not because he is a spirit, but because he is a shadow. Nothing of that real sense of the omnipresence and omnipotence of a Divine Being, which seems to possess the most stolid of settled Moslems and elevates their creed at its best into one of the purest forms of monotheism conceivable, is present to the wanderers. They are as careless of Allah as, they take it, he is careless of them. When he first made the world, say Bedawis, he ordered Creation during six days, and, very weary on the seventh, was composing himself to sleep, when a man stood before him and said: "Thou hast apportioned the world, but to us given nothing. Behold us still in the desert!"

And the Creator looked and saw the Bedawis indeed forgotten in the Waste; but he would not disturb what he had done. "This I give you," he replied; "since ye dwell in what is no man's, ye may take what is any man's. Go your way." And his way from that hour has the Bedawi gone, careless of Creation and Creator.

It was deep night still, and the moon, sinking to the sea-rim, threw an image of the tent-door across the fire, bleaching the glow of the wood embers. Little by little the pale light crept up the old dame's face. She opened her eyes suddenly as a waking animal, shuffled her knees sideways from under the man's shoulders, gently lowered his head to a saddlebag, and yawning, left the tent. I heard her gathering fuel without, with which presently she made up the fire. Then she went down towards the fold, where a continuous jangle told of uneasy udders and prescience of coming day.

The fresh warmth to my feet made me drowsy again, and when I woke once more, the dusk of dawn was in the tent, but the dame had not returned. Still milking and tending the herd, she at least showed little enough of that indolent habit with which we credit the East.

I scrambled to my feet, stiff with cramp and cold, and stood in the tent-door. The great wolf-dogs, who had bayed me over night, recognised a temporary adoption into the family by sidling silently out of range, and settling watchful again on the gossamers. During the chill hours a false impalpable sea had streamed inland, and, filling the hollow where Pátara lay, had submerged all but the higher dunes; but above its smoky limit, the true sea could be seen swelling to the horizon in palest tints of mauve and green. The profile of a shaggy range, beyond the Xanthus river, grew harder and harder against the brightening sky, rib after rib detaching itself on the ample slopes; and led upwards along its crest towards the parent chain of Taurus, my eyes caught the first flush of day on a pinnacle of snow. The old Yuruk stretched himself once or twice, rose, spat, pushed through the door, and, leaving his dame to set milk and cheese before us, strode off without a word of farewell.

The Yuruk guide of yesterday led us out northward through a triple Roman archway, and along a street of tombs. The Xanthus river rushed a mile or two to our left, red with the melted snows of Ak Dagh, and the rudely paved path wound over spongy swards and across soft reedy channels towards the neck of the plain. One would have known it for a poisonous place, even had it not earned ill-fame by killing two of Fellows' men. After an hour or two we reached a bridge, and beyond the outlet of the eastern swamp, entered a region of scattered fields, gnarled olives, and solitary farms, holdings of the "Turks" of Gunuk, who are sons of the old Lycians, county gentlemen in a small way, sportsmen always, and brigands now and then. Every man we met went armed, and the Bey, at whose house we dismounted under the steep of Xanthus, kept a guard of three.

The ruins, far seen on a sunlit slope since the first hour of our ride, lie on the first shelf of the mountains, high above the river at the point where it issues into the plain. Little seemed changed since Fellows' day, and the stakes, with which he propped the roof of the "Harpy Tomb" after stripping the frieze, still uphold it. If you feel a momentary pang of shame before the

THE DESPOILED HARPY TOMB.

Facing p. 62.

mutilated pillar, look round at the poisonous marsh and the wild hills and wilder men and you will not blame Fellows. How many artists of two generations would have seen the Harpy reliefs in their place? The Theatre, whose curve is so oddly broken to avoid a pillar-tomb, is one tangle of brushwood; but the great four-square stela, inscribed in the strange Lycian character, on all its marble faces, stands yet clear and unhurt; and you may walk eastwards from it all the length of the main street to a wide paved area, from which lesser flagged ways run right and left. The whole ground-plan of the city is there, and more of it evidently survives from the earliest days than on any other Anatolian site. Some day a digger will get a rich booty at Xanthus, and gather his first-fruits, I dare wager, on that jutting shelf shored up by cyclopean walling behind the Theatre, where a temple of the Xanthian Apollo or of Sarpedon stood as an outpost towards the sea, and struggling barley reveals, by the variety of its growth, the outline of a great oblong building. But the day of digging Xanthus seems no nearer. First Crete, and then Sparta have drawn off our explorers, and Lycia must still wait.

The ride round the eastern side of the swamp to Kalamáki I have endured twice since that day, and I know it for one of the most painful in Anatolia, so rough and broken is the paved path, and so dank the air. I shall not revive its memory. No sumptuous yacht was ever a more welcome sight than Antóni's little craft rocking in the evening light under the cliffs of Kalamáki. The south-wester had lulled at last, and we ran out before a light land breeze. We had no mind to go back to Castellórizo, unless we could do no better; for what with blockade-running in Crete, and waiting on the chance of a Turkish war, the Greek coasters could no longer be trusted to call. A week or so even in that fortunate isle would hang too heavy on our hands. So we lay to off the western point, Antóni promising to run to Rhodes, for the first time in his little boat's history, should a fair wind spring up by the next noon. As luck would have it, a north-easter began to blow at dawn, and he kept his word, as always. We woke to find the boat heeling over at racing pace with the mouth of the Xanthus astern and the bluffs of the Seven Capes sliding forward one behind another. As we hissed through the white-caps of the open gulf, I liked Antóni better than ever. He cuddled the tiller of his little boat like a lover, talking of the fame which should be hers in Castellórizo if she could run the eighty miles to Rhodes before sundown. And she did her best. The harbour was well in sight when the wind died away, leaving a light night-air to waft us, after some hours of calm, to the windmills, which have stood on the mole of Rhodes since the Hospitallers came.

In the first of the morning we heard the news—the Greeks had crossed the Thessalian border, and it was war. Some Jewish loafer on the quay must have reported that we were speaking Greek aboard; for the port authority roundly refused to accept our British passports, and set a watch over us at our inn. At the same time Antóni and his boat found themselves under arrest. It mattered little, however; for our acting consul knew me, and the Governor General of the Isles, who when *vali* of Adana had furthered my party some years before, was then in Rhodes, and had not forgotten. The embargo was lifted with a genial counsel to us not to run about the sea with Greeks till better times; and Antóni, paid as we loved him, which was well, picked up a cargo, and spread his sail for Castellórizo to tell the tale of the cruise.

CHAPTER III.

CRETE.

I RETURNED to Athens towards the end of the same year to take up the direction of the British School of Archaeology, but that task can hardly be counted among the accidents of an antiquary's life. Nor will I describe the uneventful excavation, which it fell to me to conduct in Melos, while waiting the day to put spade into a richer Aegean soil, the soil of Crete. The day came with the year 1900. The massacre of Candia forced a Great Power to rid the island for ever of the Turk; and in the spring of 1899 I accompanied the future explorer of Cnossus on my fourth visit to Crete. Arthur Evans had long laid his plans, and, with the forethought of genius, cast his bread on troubled waters by buying a Bey's part share of the site of the Palace of Minos. He seemed to waste labour and money; for under the Ottoman law his title could not be made secure, and in the end his ownership lapsed to a partner. But when others, who coveted Cnossus, put forward moral rights, he alone could urge the convincing claim of sacrifice, and the Cretans, for whom he had done much in their hour of danger, upheld his cause in the hour of freedom. We journeyed, that spring, all round the eastern half of the island, peg-

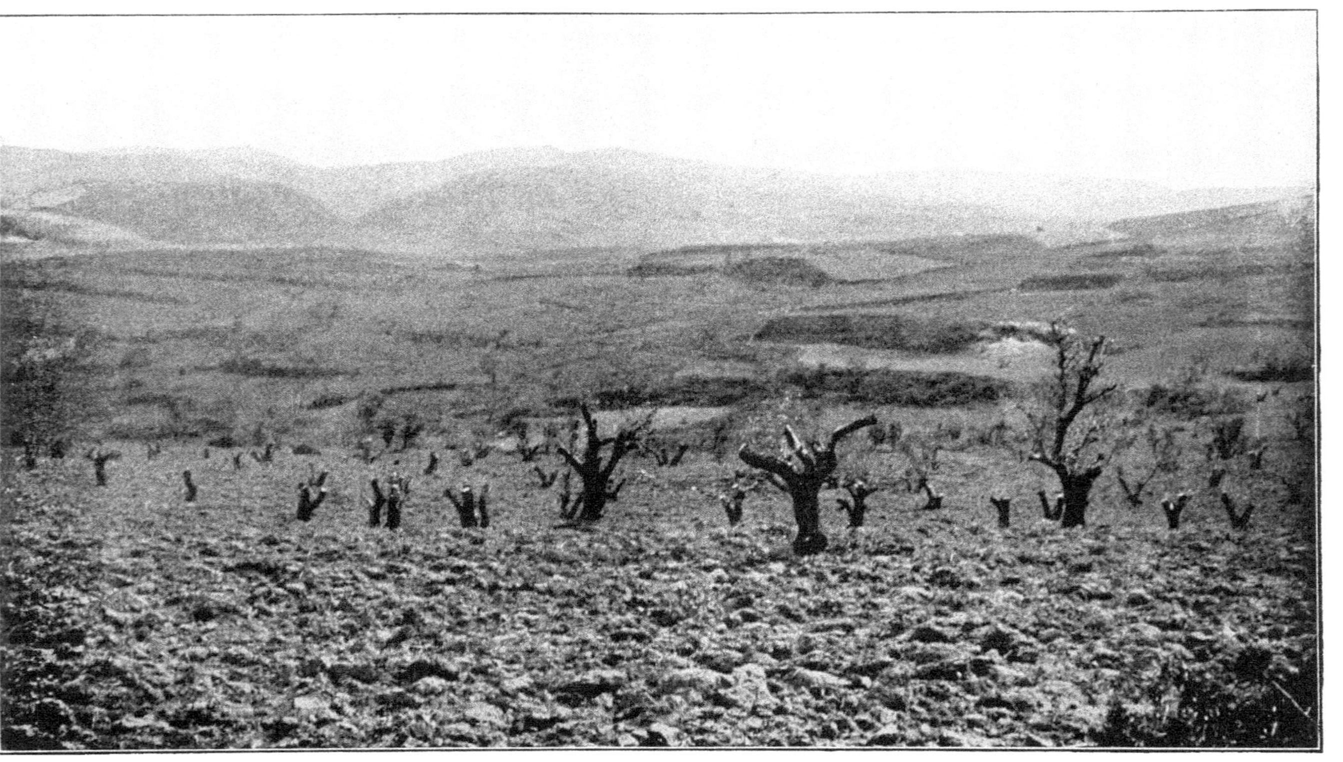

BLACKENED STUMPS AND PITS.

Facing p. 67.

ging out claims for future digging. Known to the islanders as we both were (though I the less), we were made welcome everywhere. The land still showed ghastly wounds of its late long fight. Many villages lay gaunt skeletons of ruin; and where olive groves had been, blackened stumps and pits bore witness to the ethnicidal fury of religious war in the Near East, which ever uproots the staple of a foeman's life, after it has killed the mother and her babe.

In the East of the island the French were still guiding the new rulers with the ready sympathy of Latin for Latin, and nearer to Candia the government had been committed for the moment to the honest but ruder hands of British subalterns. I spent a day or so with one of these. He knew no word of Greek, and it was told of him that when he arrived on a polo pony to be a father to some twenty villages, the local Bishop called in state, bringing, as the ingratiating custom is, a turkey or two and a clutch of eggs. Our young law-giver, nosing a bribe, put him into the street, eggs, turkey, and all I sat one morning in his court-house to hear justice done to the people. The judge presided in knickerbockers and a cricket shirt—for the day was warm—and smoked his best loved briar. A peasant, whose sheep had been driven off, had heard, after many days, a tinkling by night on a distant hillside, and claimed he knew his bells again. Did then one sheep-bell so differ from another? Solomon put it to the test. He sent his soldier servant to collect bells from the village shepherds, and on his return locked him in an inner room, while they waited in court. After a jangle behind the door, the judge asked whose bell had tinkled, and, on the witness of the servant, the shepherds were right every time. The peasant got back his sheep. Then a woman stood forth to accuse a man of trying her door by night with foul intent; but since he had neither prevailed nor spoken with her, and it was black dark, how had she known what man he was? It came out in evidence that this had not been his first visit, nor had he been used to find the door barred and the lady all unkind. Promptly he was fined a few piastres for disturbing the village peace, while the coy accuser was sent to hoe the Bishop's potato-field for a fortnight of working days. "Ah! this is Justice," said the delighted Headman to me. "We have not known it before in Crete!"

For us, then, and no others, in the following year Minos was waiting when we rode out from Candia. Over the very site of his buried Throne a desolate donkey drooped, the one living thing in view. He was driven off, and the digging of Cnossus began. All men who care for these things know by now what was revealed in the next few weeks; and it is another's right to retell the tale. I did something to help my colleague to start, for in digging, as in most ventures, the first steps are most difficult: and I did more in the following months to define the limits of his vast field, of which much still waits the spade. But it grew clearer every day that the central hillock, which in all reason was his peculiar preserve, held the key of the town's early history, and almost all its riches, and that exploration were better left undone in the outskirts until the centre had all been laid bare. Therefore I quitted Cnossus in early May, and with Gregóri of Cyprus, who was still following my fortunes after a dozen years, set out eastwards for the second of our claims, a Cave which was suspected to be the mythic birthplace of the Father God of Crete.

In our theology He, who shall be to all time, from all time has been; but the Greek, conceiving Immortality more easily than Eternity, branded the Cretans the liars of antiquity for showing on one hill the tomb of Zeus, while he believed devoutly in the divine birthplace, which was pointed out on another. Other lands, indeed, claimed the honour; but the beautiful peaks, which rose in pale mornings and opalescent evenings out of the southern sea, prevailed with the Faithful. If, however, the Greek was sure of the island to which he owed his God, he was not, in his latter days at least, so sure which precise spot had been hallowed by the divine birth. The God was certainly cradled in a cave; but there were two caves, the one in the central peak of Ida, the other in the lower but still majestic easterly mountain group of Dicte. Some, like the Sicilian Diodorus, who knew these rival claims, tried to reconcile them by telling that the babe, born on Dicte, was reared on Ida. But more voted for one or the other hill, and those of the best authority for Dicte. There the birth was placed by Hesiod, the eldest poet who relates the story; there, too, by the great Romans, Lucretius and Virgil, to say nothing of lesser lights.

This Greek tale, become more familiar to the West than many myths of its own primitive creeds, varies little in the authorities. Cronus, King of Heaven, warned that a son shall cast him from his realm, determines to devour his male issue as soon as born. But Queen Rhea, wrathful and feeling her hour nigh, flees to Crete, and on Dicte is delivered of a boy, whom she hides in a cave, while the blind old god swallows a stone in place of his child (and ever since stones have been mansions of godhead in the Near East). The baby's whimpering is drowned by the clashing shields of faithful servants or, as one story has it, by the grunting of a fostering sow. In Hesiod's narrative all this story concerns the city of Lyttus. Thither the pregnant queen was sent by the kindly Earth Mother to wait her time, and thence she set forth by night to bear in a cave of the neighbouring mountain a babe who would find the same cave convenient in later days. For thither, as Lucian tells us in his best manner, he led the maiden Europa, flushed and half suspecting ; and there too the son, whom she conceived that day, would seek his Father when, another Moses, he wished to be the Lawgiver of his people. While the Cretans waited above (so runs the story), Minos descended into this Holy Grot, and when he reappeared with the Code, gave out he had it of Zeus himself.

A primitive sanctuary was to be looked for, therefore, in some grot on Dicte, and by preference near Lyttus, whose scattered ruin lies on a spur of the north-western Lasithi peak, which is still climbed by a yearly pilgrimage and called the Lord's Mountain. In so well defined an area such a cave, if any there were, must have been identified long ago, had the upland fastnesses of Crete been any place for the scholarly explorer these many centuries past. But the Lasithi region, which excluded the Venetians and only once admitted the Turks in arms, long remained less known than even the rest of the island, and nothing was heard by the outer world of any cavern in Dicte till less than thirty years ago.

At last reports reached Candia touching a large double grot which is seen as a black spot on the hill-side above Psychró, a village of the inner Lasithi plain. It was said that shepherds, folding their flocks in it at night or in storm, had grubbed up strange objects of bronze and terra-cotta from the black bottom mould. Their finding continued, and three years later the first archaeologists came to Psychró and recovered divers antiques from peasant hands—figurines of men and beasts, miniature battle axes, knives and other weapons. They climbed, moreover, to the Cave itself, and scraped away the earth from its mouth in vain hope of uncovering such an altar as had existed without the Zeus grot on Ida; but inside they found little to do, so heavy was the cumber of fallen rocks in the upper hall. What they had recovered, however, was plainly part of a votive deposit, and the cave was marked holy and a prize for explorers to come.

To Psychró, therefore, I betook myself with a few trained men, some stone-hammers, mining-bars, blasting powder, and the rest of a cave-digger's plant. The villagers proved willing, nay eager, belying my fear that a cold reception awaited anyone who came to poach this preserve of illicit searchers. Just then Lasithi, like all Crete, was anxious before all things to justify its new won freedom in European eyes, and Psychró was not less alive than any other Greek village would have been, to the glory to be shed on its little self by notable discoveries in its Cave. Furthermore, from week to week the Prince High Commissioner was expected in Lasithi. He had announced he would visit the Cave, and here in the nick of time was an Englishman offering to make, at his own charges, the needful path for the royal mules. Therefore, on a stormy morning, while the hillside was swept by clammy mists and half-frozen showers, I found no lack of hands to make me a zig-zag mule-track up five hundred feet of rock. Knowing that the path would serve them thereafter to bring down the black cave mould, which the farmers of the plain prize above all top-dressings, the Psychró men finished it in less than a day; and while a camping ground was being levelled and embanked before the yawning mouth, we began to blast a way into the cave itself.

Let it be understood that this great cavern is double, having a shallow hall to right, and an abysmal chasm to left, which is not unworthy to rank among the famous limestone grottoes of the world. The rock falls sheer at first, but, as the light grows dim, you find your feet on an easier slope, and can clamber down safely into deeper darkness. Having groped thus far, stand and burn a flare. In front an icy pool spreads from your feet far into the hill about the bases of fantastic stalactite columns, and hall opens out of hall, each with fretted roof and black unruffled floor, while behind and far above a spot of luminous haze shows the way you have come from the upper world. It is a fit scene for Minos' colloquy with his father Zeus, and for the cult of a chthonian God. To-day the hill-girt plain of Lasithi, laid level as a sand beach, drains to a stream which is sucked into darkness below an overhanging cliff, and reappears, perhaps, in certain large springs which rise among the northern roots of the hills; but its floor, which is seen now from above as a huge chequer-board, has not always been dry. A lake, lapping the mountain flanks five hundred feet above, once poured its overflow into the hill through the Cave of Psychró, and made it such a natural marvel as would appeal to the superstition of primitive peasants.

Blasting powder made short work of the boulders in the upper hall, whose threatening roof held good to the end, and crowbars and stone-hammers finished the work. In four strenuous days we had not only hewn a path into the upper hall, but cleared a large area of black mould, and the real search could begin. But preparations for further blasts had still to go on, with an incessant ringing of mining bars; and what with their metallic din, reverberating from roof to walls, what with the heavy hanging fumes of powder and the mingled reek of hot, unwashed men and chill, newly turned earth, we had not too pleasant a task in that dim, dripping cave. All soil was carried out of the dark up the steep incline, and to sifting it and washing the blackened potsherds it contained was set a gang of women, who are always more patient in minute search than men, and less apt to steal. It is always well to have a few women among your diggers. The men labour better in their company, and with a vivacity which is of no small value where boredom spells failure. The day, which else might drag its slow length along, goes merrily in chatter and laughter, and the task is sought cheerfully at dawn, and not willingly left at eve. As a master of labour, I have met with least reluctance from women in Moslem lands. The Bedawi wives of the northern half tribe of Walad Ali, which has settled about the mounds of Gaif in the Nile Delta during the last fifty years, came without the least demur to help their husbands and brothers dig Naukratis. They even brought their sucklings; and on the first day more than one mother tried to carry her basket of earth on one shoulder, while a brown babe nestled at her breast. As the poor mite received a deluge of sand in mouth and eyes whenever the load was tipped unhandily, I forbade babies in arms for the morrow; but no one seemed to understand why. In Cyprus, too, Turkish mothers flocked to our work, and their little girls, enlisted more for the pleasure of the sight of them than anything else, used to turn the Paphian Temple into a riotous playground. But Eastern Christians are usually more prudish or more fearful, and I had expected that no Lasithi woman would work. Sure enough they proved coy, and at first would only watch from afar two trained girls brought up from Cnossus as lures; but on the third morning a cosmopolitan villager, who had fought—or looted—in France in 1870, sent up his wife and a daughter to help his son, and the ice was broken. A laughing mob ran up the hill tossing sieves and clamouring to be listed, and with their sisters, cousins and aunts, who brought up the midday meals, made the terrace before our cave the gayest spot in Lasithi.

Above a thick bed of yellow clay, laid long ago by water, and productive only of bones and scraps of very primitive pottery, lay black earth five to seven feet deep at the back of the Upper Hall. It proved to hold countless burned things, and, also, many unburned offerings, which had been laid or dropped at all periods, from about the early classical age back to a dim antiquity, roughly coeval with the Twelfth Dynasty of Pharaohs. Bronzes from many moulds were hidden there, a little chariot, for example, drawn by an ox and a ram, unequally yoked; many miniature effigies of bulls and sheep; knives, pins, lance-heads, needles, and little necessaries of the toilet; and also hundreds of clay cups, and some finely painted potter's work, and rough libation tables of stone. These lay thickest about a rude structure, bedded on the yellow clay, which was doubtless an altar of burnt sacrifice. The dark innermost recess, shut off by a rough and ruinous wall, was long shunned; for the rock-roof was unsound above it, and great fragments overhung perilously. But when we ventured into it at the last, nothing worse happened than sudden thunderous slides of rock and earth, which at first sent the scared diggers scampering for their lives, but soon came to be held harmless. This sacrosanct area was soil untouched by the modern searcher, and it proved extraordinarily prolific in broken vases, mostly of painted ware, but less rich in metal things. To clear the whole Upper Hall took no more than a fortnight; and I was well enough pleased on the whole when I gave it back to its fluttered bats and owls. The altar and temenos wall had proved the place holy, and nothing less, in all likelihood, than the Birth Cave itself.

It remained, however, to search the Lower Hall for objects that might have slipped down during the secret digging of the past fifteen years; but I did not expect much spoil, since I was told that no native had ever found anything among these dim stalactite pillars except a few scraps of water-borne pottery. Unwilling and not hopeful, the men clambered down into the abyss, and the women especially, who had been working hitherto in sunshine at the Cave's mouth, moaned at sight of the clammy mud in which they must now stand and search by the smoky light of petroleum flares. But complaints soon ceased, as first one and then another picked a bronze out of the soil which had lodged on the upper rock slopes. Two objects among the handfuls which I was called to collect from time to time were especially welcome, one a little statuette of the god of Egyptian Thebes, Amen Ra (how came he there? in the hand of an Egyptian or a Cretan devotee?); the other a miniature battle-axe, earnest of more to come.

There was not room, however, for all hands on the steep slope, and I bade a few of the best workers rake out the little pockets of lime-encrusted mud, which had been laid in cups and hollows on the lower stalagmitic floors. There, too, blades and pins were found; and, working down and down into the darkness, till their distant lights shone no brighter than glow-worm lamps to the men above, the pioneers reached the margin of the subterranean pool, and began to scrape the mud-slides left by the water as it shrinks in summer time into the hill. So much did this slime yield that some went on unbidden to dredge the shallows of the chill pool itself, and find there many rude bronze statuettes, male and female, nude and draped, vicarious deputies of worshippers who had wished to be specially remembered of the God, and also signet gems and rings, pins, needles by the score.

By this time more than half the workfolk were splashing in the nether pool, eager for the special rewards promised to lucky finders; and the tale of bronzes had already been doubled. But Chance had reserved her crowning grace. A zealous groper, wishful to put both hands to his work, happened to wedge his guttering candle in the fluting of a stalactite column, and by its light espied in the slit the green edge of a bronze blade. I passed the word to leave mud-larking in the pool and search the colonnades. Men and girls dispersed themselves along the dark aisles, and perching above the black waters on natural crockets of the pillars, peered into the flutings. They found at once—found blades, pins, tweezers, brooches, and here and there a votive axe, and in some niches as many as ten votive things together. Most were picked out easily enough by the slim fingers of the girls; but to possess ourselves of others, which the lights revealed, it was necessary to smash stalactite lips that had almost closed in long ages. For about four hours we discovered at least an object a minute, chiefly on the columns at the head of the pool: but above the stature of a man nothing was anywhere found.

When nothing more could be seen in the crevices, which had been scrutinised twice and thrice, and we had dredged the pool's bed as far as wading men could reach, I called off the workers, who were falling sick of the damp and chill; and two days later we left silent and solitary the violated shrine of the God of Dicte. The digger's life is a surfeit of surprises, but his imagination has seldom been provoked so sharply as in that dim chasm. One seemed to come very near indeed to men who lived before history. As we saw those pillared isles, so with little change had the last worshipper, who offered a token to Zeus, seen them three thousand years ago. No later life had obliterated his tracks; and we could follow them back into the primaeval world with such stirring of fancy as one feels in the Desert, which is the same to-day as it was yesterday, and has been since the beginning of things.

I have never struck tents with sharper regret, for there could be no pleasanter abode than a camp on that rocky shelf of Dicte. All day handsome folk went and came, who dealt as honourably with the stranger as he wished to deal with them, showing neither distrust nor presumption, but a frank highland gentility; and as evening fell, they would turn merrily down the hill, only lingering to exchange a word or to load a mule with soil for the gardens below. By night we were alone, free and irresponsible as Bedawis, and far safer; for in that distressful isle of Crete, where every peasant had his tale of rapine and murder in his own or his father's time, there was no suspicion of fear. Sometimes the scourge of the Cretan spring, a hot Libyan gust, would swoop unheralded from the higher gullies, and set the cook's coals scurrying towards the big powder canister and himself in frantic chase, calling on the Virgin Mother; and half a dozen times it seemed our tents must go by the sheer way to the village, whose lights twinkled five hundred feet below. But poles and ropes held out against the worst of the wind, and soon the moon rode in cloudless heaven once more, and the flags drooped motionless on their standards. So the night would pass, and with the dawn the chatter be heard again, coming round the shoulder of the hill.

A year later I was camped still further east on the uttermost Cretan coast which looks towards the Levant sea. Broken pieces of painted vases had been found some time before about the mouth of a large pit near a little natural harbour, now known as the Bay of Zakro; and the vineyards of a little hamlet on the lower slopes were embanked with walls of primaeval masonry. The bay was much frequented. Often one waked to find a dozen or so of small craft

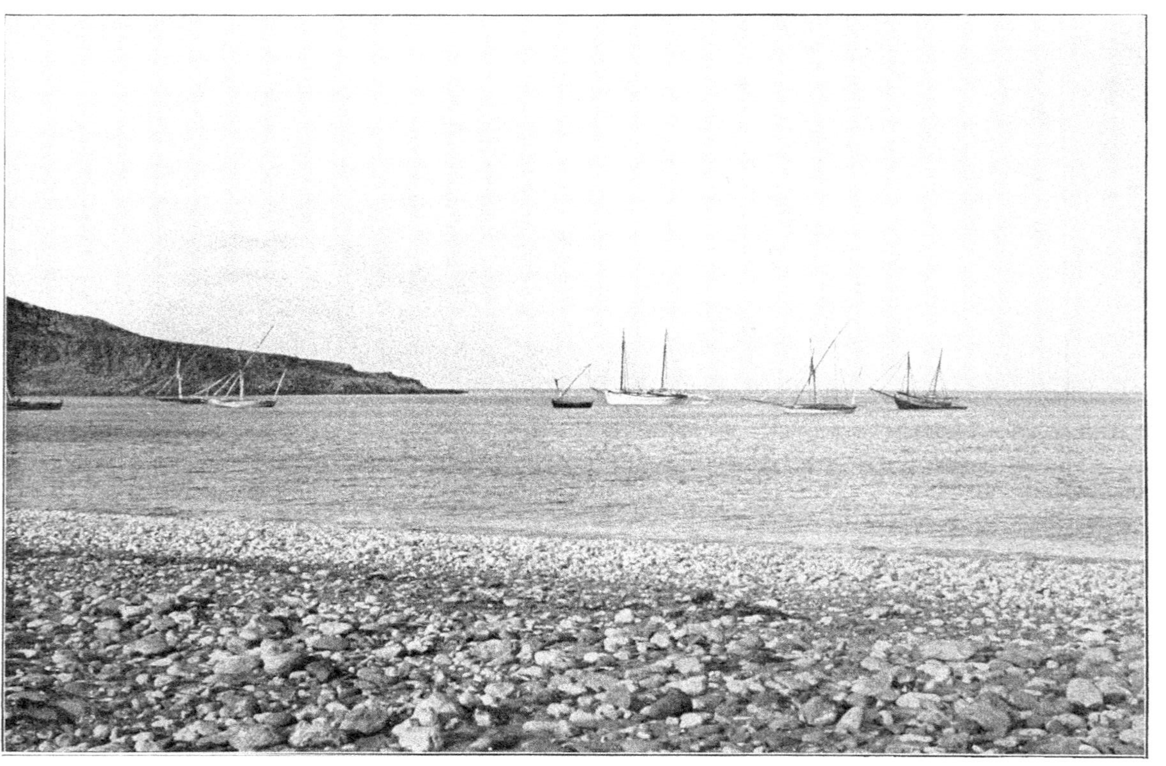

SPONGE BOATS IN ZAKRO BAY.

Facing p. 79.

at anchor, whose sailors would land in the morning to draw water, seek the blessing of a priest, and be gone after noon. Some came to talk with me, and declared themselves strangers, sponge-divers, gathered from many coasts, but chiefly from the Isle of Symi. They were men of swarthy skin, somewhat boisterous and given to drinking and dicing,—bent on a merry life, because in their trade it is short. Zakro, said they, was their last customary port of call before they adventured over the broad strait to the Libyan fishing grounds. As they do now, so Cretans must have done in the days of Minos; and by trade Zakro grew so rich nearly four thousand years ago that it possessed some of the finest vases in the Aegean, and became cosmopolitan enough to use the products of Syria and inner Asia.

I began to search my ground and reached the fourteenth of May by our reckoning, the second in the older style. The weather had been boisterous for a fortnight past, and under some unseasonable influence shifting gales, lowering skies, and frequent rains had succeeded the serenity of April. A heavier fall than usual began in the afternoon, and during the windless early hours of night grew to a tropical deluge. I was encamped in front of a large magazine, the only building upon the beach, about a quarter of a mile from the mouth of a river which comes down from the upland shelves of Sitía. The noble gorge of its middle course, cleft sheer as a Pacific cañon, was set so thick with old trees and tangled undergrowth, when I saw it first, that a man could scarcely pass along its floor; in the broad upper valley above high-water mark, cornplots, orchards, and terraced gardens flourished abundantly, and the deltaic plain about the mouth was even more fertile still.

Presently I had to abandon the tent, though it had been proof against former rains, and seek sleep in the rat-ridden magazine. Its mud roof was leaking apace, and the four dripping walls dismally reflected the lamp-light; but, thankful for even such shelter, I fell asleep. I woke to hear fierce hissing of wind and rain driven on the sea-front of the building, and by the roaring of breakers knew that an onshore gale had risen during the night. It was grey-dark, and, striking a light to see how long it might still be to sunrise, I wondered to find the hour past already, and day dismally come.

For lack of anything better to do, I tried to sleep again; but my Greek servants, moving restlessly about the building, infected me with their uneasiness. Though the magazine was built on shingle and sand, it lay so far out of the course in which the river had flowed for centuries, that there could hardly be danger where we were, however damp our discomfort. But that untimely gloom, riven by the fitful shimmer of lightning, that steady splash of rain, reinforced by cascades of driven sea-spray, and that intermittent thunder, which could be heard even above the ceaseless roar of breakers rolling to my threshold, were not heartening. Water stood deep on the plain behind; but it was finding its own outlets to the sea, and I took more heed of the deluge overhead, which so thoroughly penetrated the mud roof, that there was nothing for it but to disturb the careful order of stores and baggage, and the results of my digging, and collect all under waterproof sheets in the middle of the magazine.

I was making a cold and sodden breakfast, when I heard suddenly a shout, "The river! The river!" I splashed outside, and, wading to the south end of the long windowless building, saw that the flooded surface of the plain behind had begun to flow as one stream. Torrents, growing momentarily stronger and deeper, swept round each end of the magazine, under-cutting its shallow foundations; and even as I looked, a crack ran like a lightning fork down the masonry of the north end. It opened ever so little, and I watched my kitchen slide into the flood noiselessly; for nothing was to be heard above the roaring of sky and sea. It was high time to be gone. In the farther chamber of the magazine a mare was standing, but mad with terror of the lightning and the water, she would not budge, even when one wall of her stable followed the kitchen, and after a frantic struggle she had to be left to her fate. I plunged with the stable boy into the northern mill-race and staggered through; but the overseer and the cook, who lingered a moment to search for a much-loved pinfire gun under the ruins of the kitchen, found the water already too deep and strong, and had to wait for a life-line; whereof the cook lost his hold, and was all but swept to the sea. Fortunately, the higher ground was not far distant, and to it we all fled.

For the next two hours, wet to the skin—and feeling, too, as if wet from skin to skin—we had to crouch in what shelter we might, and watch the ruin of the valley. The deluge from the skies never abated a moment, and the solid earth seemed to melt. Where yesterday a foot-fall had rung on the flinty hillside, one now sank ankle-deep. The very heart of the storm was hanging over us. Lightnings forked ceaselessly on one hand or the other, and each thunder-peal confused the echo of the last. The gale, a full-bodied "Levanter," was still freshening; and under its awful lash the seas, stained red with the ruin of the fields, reared higher and higher against the boiling race which the land was pouring in. The river now filled the whole valley from hill to hill, here sliding with swift, malignant smoothness, there, broken by some obstacle or penned in a sunken gully, heaving, shouldering, writhing and tossing turbid waves one across the other. Gnarled planes and centenarian holm-oaks from the river gorge, with olives and charubs, which told the fate of the higher gardens and orchards, rode past us in an endless tumult—all horribly tangled with horned carcasses, which were sucked spinning below, to be spewed up again and swept to the sea. It was a Homeric combat between two floods. Great trees, hurled into the jaws of the breakers, reared, plunged, and broke back like hunted monsters of the deep; till at last, where the forces of propulsion and resistance neutralised each other offshore, they gathered in an ever-broadening vortex and still found no peace.

During the last hour of the storm the gale seemed to master all the other cataclysmal forces. The southern point of the bay, where a reef sheers up in jagged iron cliffs, provoked the most horrid turmoil; and, above all rival sounds of land and sky, came down wind a ceaseless roar of riotous seas, leaping to the summit of the rocks. Two misty trails streamed far inland like smoke from chimney stacks on the summit of the cliff. They were, of course, two storm-cataracts caught in their leap and whirled to spray; but the Cretans, who watched with me, finding any wonder credible in that convulsion of all nature, would have it the central fires of earth had broken out, and I doubt not they still add that crowning portent to their tales of an unforgotten day.

While the tremendous spectacle continued, none of us gave much thought to his own miserable state. We cowered watching how primaeval earth was carved. When the veil of rain was withdrawn at last, I saw the whole face of the landscape changed. The old estuary of the river existed no more; and a broad and shallow mouth had been opened far to the north. The bay, which since Spratt's visit in the 'fifties had afforded deep anchorage close inshore, now shoaled gradually for a mile, and was studded with the toppling crests of grounded trees; and the mile-long strand of pebbles and grassy dunes had been replaced by a stretch of mud at a level some six feet lower. Over two-thirds of the plain, where fertile fields and olive gardens had been, lay sand and stones; and such trees as had held their ground were buried to mid-trunk. Looking up the river gorge, I saw nothing but naked rock, where terraced vineyards had clothed the cliff face; while all the ancient tangle of forest below had vanished to the last shrub, and the sinuous valley-floor, as far as the eye could follow it, glistened clean as a city pavement after rain.

When the flood had subsided, a part of the shell of my magazine was found standing, saved by the yielding of the beach to right and left; and the mare, quite unhurt, shivered still in the only remaining corner of her roofless stable. My personal loss was not so very great. I had to find new quarters, repair much that was broken, and put up with the loss of many stores and utensils, but of nothing absolutely indispensable to the camp. But if I had come off lightly on the whole, not so had the natives of the valley. Its single village, when the Headman came to make his official report, was found to have lost thousands of fruit-trees, many score head of live stock, and a number of houses and farm buildings. Communication with the rest of the island was cut by the washing out of paths, made with the labour of years; and the best springs of drinking water were smothered under a landslip. Since all irrigated fields and gardens whatsoever, which had been terraced along the stream, had been swept away, the villagers had lost not only the crops of the year, nor only the fruit of their trees for several years to come, nor only the trees themselves, but also the precious, irretrievable soil on which there could be growth again. The sum of their disaster came to this. Almost all members of a community of poor husbandmen, who had nothing but their lands to look to, had lost in a few hours all that they possessed over and above the barest means of subsistence. For many years to come they would have no more than the scanty produce of their higher and thinner fields to live upon. If none would starve, thanks to the communism of Eastern society, none would be able to grow for himself, or have the means to procure, a seasoning of his daily bread. The slow increase of many generations past was lost to a generation to come. The village, as it seemed to me, was ruined.

Cut off all that day by the river, we could only guess what had happened in the upper valley; but on the morrow two or three of the villagers, who had held lands in the lower plain, forded the falling stream at their peril, and came down to us. Their tale set one's imagination playing over the dull hopelessness of their outlook, over this state of men, yesterday prosperous to-day face to face with the prospect of a bitter, inevitable struggle for mere bread, their hope of joy in life abandoned, and their local pride, so keenly felt in Greek village society, for ever abased. To my Western thinking such a fate seemed worse than death. Could nothing be done? I was the single individual in the valley with any superfluity, and I represented a foreign Society, whose duty and right it was to help. If I could not recover their trees or put back their soil, I could still do what the Briton always does in such emergencies—write a cheque. So word was sent up to the Headman that I proposed to offer a certain sum to the village, if he would tell me how it would be spent.

Next day the lower ford was just passable, and I rode across country—for the path was gone—to see what I might. Every glimpse into the gorge from above showed how completely vanished was its ancient forest, the most valuable and rare possession of a Cretan village. As the valley opened out and our way lay through the wrecked olive gardens, now dreary stretches of drying mud, on whose caked surface sand was beginning to swirl in the breeze, I saw that the tree-stumps were banked up on their higher side with a matted scum of broken boughs, of corn uprooted in the green ear and of other ruin of the valley lands; while stranded boulders and stones were strewn so thick on once fertile fields as to make all seem one broad river-bed.

In the village I found several houses destroyed, and men still labouring to clear others of the mud left by the collapse of their roofs. I was invited to go on to the Mill and see what evil work the flood had done there. The coffee-house emptied itself behind me of some twenty men, to whom were added presently half the women and children of the village, all surprisingly cheerful, and vying with one another to be first in pointing out this or that result of the disaster. God had willed it! So each murmured piously at the end of a tale, which lost nothing in the manner of its telling. The principal sufferers were brought forward, and were plainly proud to be so distinguished. They, too, said modestly that God had willed it. The mill proved to be no more; and the miller pointed out its situation with so manifest a pleasure that I almost suspected, absurdly enough, that the blessing of excessive insurance was not unknown in remote Cretan villages.

Returned to the coffee-house, I found still less to feed a pitiful mood. Seven men in ten of the company were there, because they had no longer any lands to till; but the outward demeanour of each and all was not that which one looked for in despairing men. Nor, if I am any judge of behaviour (and these were very simple folk), was the heart of the Zakriotes heavy within them, while they talked so cheerfully. The story of the day before yesterday was told again and again, with fresh effects added to taste, and always with that pious refrain about the will of God—a story of something past and done with, no longer taken into account for the present or the future.

I rose with emotion not a little chastened, and went to the Headman. He was writing out his report to the local prefecture, and laid down his pen to relate with sparkling eyes the narrow escape of his own family from a torrent which had come right through a house higher up the hill-side. But when I referred to my proposed gift, he showed less interest. If I had looked to play Lord Bountiful in Zakro, I had missed my mark. The man was evidently as much embarrassed as grateful. It was not easy, he said, to spend such a sum on the village as a whole. None was worse off than another. All were poor men. What did I wish to do myself? The church would be the better for a belfry. I was taken aback, having proposed to myself something of more eleemosynary sort. Or should the water of a certain spring be brought down in pipes? Neither was this just what I had expected; but caring more to add to fountains in a thirsty land than to ecclesiastical luxuries, I voted for the pipes, and handed over my dole, not so much, after all, in pity for stricken men as dislike to be worse than my word.

Those peasants had, perhaps, feigned a little, as a Greek will, half unconsciously, if there be a chance to plume himself, even on misery. But I saw and heard much of them after their excitement had long passed and they were grown both familiar with me and fully aware of the measure of their loss; yet still undismayed, they held on their simple way after, as before a disaster which would have crushed or maddened northern husbandmen. Nor was their mood either callous or light. The peasant Greek is neither brute nor butterfly; but this he is—a man who is essentially inert, a man born physically outworn. The whole race, as it seems to me, is suffering from over-weariness. It lived fast in the forefront of mankind very long ago, and now is far gone in years; and in its home you feel that you have passed into the shadow of what has been, into an air in which men would rather be than do.

No doubt, also, the passivity common to most tillers of the earth reinforced the inborn nature of the Zakriotes.

The husbandman is of all men the most apt to surrender to the discretion of Heaven and take its blows without thought whether they be deserved. Slave of the soil which he turns, to it he looks for all his being. What it gives him from year to year may vary in degree but not in kind. Much or little, it is always food. To be poor or rich is to have his belly better filled or worse; and, eating to live, he lives to eat only on a rare day of festival. So his customary toil, than which he knows no other business of his day, give him enough food, the shortening of it, or the loss of its variety will affect him less than a being of less simple life would think possible. Actual starvation he has not felt, and knows he will never feel, so long as his neighbour has food. His joys are found, not outside his day's work, but in its course—in the satisfaction of bodily appetite, in drinking when he is athirst, in sleeping when he is weary, in warming himself in God's sun, in cooling himself in the shade, in communing with his fellows, his wife and his babes. What should such a man know of the superfluity which we call wealth?

Simple though the Zakriotes were, they showed often in their talk that they knew themselves well enough to be preoccupied with this very question of their racial decay. Why, they were for ever asking me, had the Greeks fallen out of that front rank in which the schoolmaster told them they once marched? How came the "barbarians" of Europe to be now, nation for nation and man for man, so superior to the once Chosen Race? The processes of generation and birth, processes which, whether in man or beast, are never out of the thoughts or the talk of southern folk, were canvassed to show cause. Their maidens, they said, were betrothed as children, wedded at fourteen, and mothers in the course of months. They had heard we discouraged wedlock before the age of sixteen. Had they not better do so too? There was talk of a League of Hellenic Ladies to promote mature marriage, and the Headman's wife, who twirled her spindle and bore her waterpot aloft among the rest, but with a statelier grace, wished to join it. Zakro had long been famous among Cretan villages for the easy delivery of mothers. A woman was not held to have done herself credit there if she let the midwife be in time. But what did I think? Did such easy bearing mean weak babes? I told the Headman's lady how hardly it went with the delicate mothers of my own land, and she scarcely believed. Like Bedawis, who will halt but an hour on the march while a wife is delivered behind a spear-propped screen of cloaks, so too the sedentary mothers of the Near East make little trouble of bringing to birth. John Barker, consul in Aleppo, tells how once he halted with his wife for the night among the Syrian hills at a hut, whose mistress was plainly very near her time. In the morning the housewife gathered the family linen to wash it at the stream a thousand feet below, and, deaf to the English lady's protests, went off down the hill. At sunset her figure was seen coming slowly up the path again, the new-washed linen on her head, the new-born babe in the crook of her arm.

I keep a very kindly memory of Zakro, despite its water fouled by the flood, despite the stenches which came up from the lightly sanded carcasses, despite the myriad mosquitoes of its shore. There was a tepid sea to bathe in morn and eve; there were fair slopes, unpeopled but not too wild, to ride over on Sabbaths and holidays; there was peace from the post and the political Greek; and there were half a score of buried brick houses of Minoan time to be explored, with all their contents, as well as pits and tombs and caves, which yielded me their secrets. I stayed till it was high summer, and what were left of barley fields were ripe already to harvest.

CHAPTER IV.

NILE FENS.

THE Delta is unvisited by the thousands who seek their pleasure winter by winter on the Nile, although a glimpse of the fringe of its fens is everyone's earliest and most vivid impression of Egypt. As the train speeds south from Alexandria, a vista slips past of level mere and copper-green fields and ant-hill villages breaking the line of an amber sky ; or, more at leisure, between Port Said and Ismailia, you may look from the hurricane-deck over a silent lagoon, with flocks of waders standing at gaze, or trailing like far-blown smoke across the setting sun.

Twice I have gone for a sojourn of some weeks into the western fens, to glean, after another's harvesting, on the mounds of Gaif, where King Amasis once made the Greeks build a very naughty city. It is a water-logged, ill-smelling spot, whose every detail is ugly or mean ; but the large sunlit spaces around made one careless of the foreground, and even in this the eye was content with the shapely Walad Ali thieves who roam the mounds, and, if one lodged at the sheikh's of the northern hamlet, with his daughter, Ayesha. She was as wild a maid as ever scoured pans for a Coptic cook and served two dusty diggers at their meat. Hers were the features of a Scopas head, the eyes of a frightened hare, and the wrists, hands, ankles, and feet of the purest breed of man. She was tattooed on brow and cheek and chin; the hue of her only robe was a smear of all the cakes in a paintbox; and she would rarely speak. When she did break silence, it was to ask for something in coin or kind towards the dowry, for lack of which she was aging at eighteen. The last time I visited Gaif, I heard she had been lifted at length to a bridal bower on camel-back, and had followed a Bedawi lord to the desert, as a sheikh's daughter should. All luck and love be with her!

I had visited the fens, however, before I saw Gaif, having once ridden into them from Alexandria, when I was ranging the neighbourhood for buried Greek cities. Much was being said then of a mound lying beyond the swamps of Mariut, in a district almost without villages—a desolate doubtful tract of sour desert fringe, through which a pioneer canal had lately been dug. Some kind of farm was said to exist near this *tell*, tenanted by a party of Frenchmen; and no sooner had the good offices of an Alexandrian friend made me known to one of them, than I was bade cordially to come as I was and stay as long as I pleased. The farm-hands should attend me, cook for me and dig, and camels and Arab steeds were waiting my pleasure. But I caught the accent of Tarascon, and when I left Alexandria a few days later, it was with both horses and a servant of my own.

A dislocated omnibus train put me down at a shed in the marsh-land, whence a path led westward through cultivated lands, and among hamlets, standing high on their proper ruin. After a halt at noon beneath a stunted palm, we passed into a region where man still

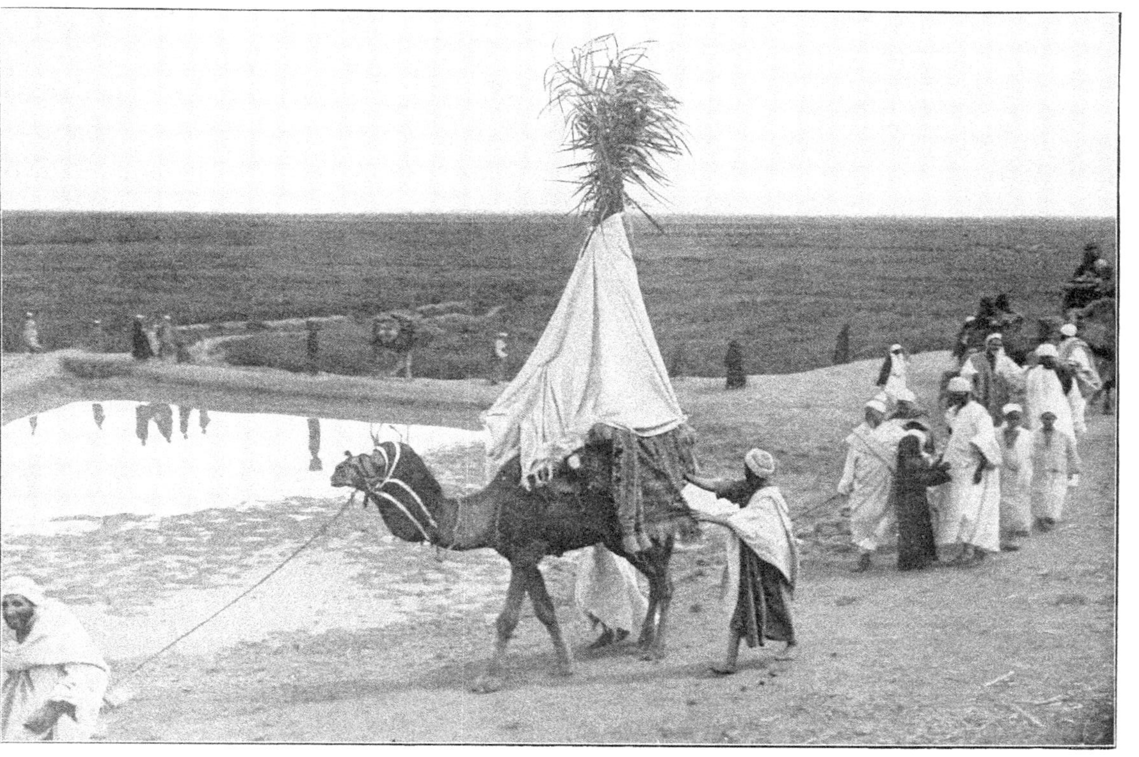

A BRIDAL BOWER AT GAIF.

Facing p. 92.

fought a drawn battle with sand and water. Here he has won a long stretch, embanked it, washed it, and raised clover and cotton in triumph; but there the salt flood has slopped into his canal, and ridge and furrow are once more barren sand.

After a while, flakes of mud began to appear among the green. The ditches, fringed with salt growths and clogged with weed, spread themselves out more frequently in muddy sloughs, and at last the main canal died away in a chain of rank reedy hollows. *Fellahin* yielded place to rare Bedawi goat-herds, and mud hovels to their black tents, pitched sparsely on sand-spits or dusty *tells*. The Frenchmen's house soon loomed in sight, set high above the vast level on one of these mounds; but not far short of it the path broke off at a black and unbridged drain, and when we had found a crossing, and floundered through the slime to the gate of the compound, it wanted but two hours to sunset. My friend's mares, mules, and camels were evidently out at pasture, for through the frequent gaps in the mud wall I could see no more than a rotting cart, some hens standing forlorn on greasy islets, and a few ducks more at their ease. The farm-house cried aloud for repair. Its roof gaped; in the windows was more paper than glass; and the balcony would not have borne up a dog. The gate of a shaggy garden swung wide on one hinge, and we clattered in unremarked by so much as a cat. No human being was visible, and as none answered to knock or call, I pushed the door, and found myself in a room of all work. The table showed that here, as in Wonderland, there was no time to wash teacups between meals; nor, apparently, had a figure, sitting somnolent beside it, with bandaged head and eye, and a torn shirt and ragged breeches for all its clothing, had more time to wash itself. The strange being blinked a single bloodshot eye, staggered to its feet, and regarded me unsteadily. Then intelligence dawned, and yelling, "Jules! Jules!" it seized me by hand and waist, and asked with affectionate solicitude what I would take—wine, beer, cognac, or champagne? A glance at the bottle on the table suggested a more local liquor. My host was hurt. Why not beer or champagne? Well, if it must be *mastica*, there it was of Scio, the best. And in his own cloudy glass he presented me with sheer unabashed potato spirit, which, taken unwarily, grips the gullet and deprives one of speech or breath.

A clatter of loose heels on the stairs heralded Jules. It was my little friend of Alexandria, evidently just out of bed. As I shook his hand I heard a gurgling sound behind, and was conscious that the common glass had been filled and emptied again. Jules placed his bed at my disposal, sheets and all, as they were, and apparently as they had been for many nights. Victor passed the *raki* repeatedly, and drank a glass for every one I refused. Both upbraided me in chorus for having brought horses, where those animals were as the sand of the sea in multitude. But none the less, on visiting the compound at sundown to seek a standing for my animals, I found a single weedy mare in the one shed, and various windy proposals resulted in my stallion being tethered to the decadent cart in the open. Presently he freed himself, and, being foiled in a gallant effort to reach the mare through the roof of her shed, took incontinently to the marsh, and amused four Bedawi catchers until the moon rose. Two days later, when I wanted an extra baggage animal, I moved heaven and earth, and hardly obtained one mangy camel.

In the meanwhile, if only to stem the tide of alcohol I had proposed to Jules that he should show me the *tell*, which rose hard by the farm. He replied that it stretched as far as the eye could see, and that to enumerate the marvellous things upon it would take the night; but, if I wished it, we might go as far as the foot. The path led through a group of Bedawi hovels, backed against the wall of the compound. There, said Jules, dwelt his men; but the manner of the retainers' salute did not savour of feudal respect. A hurried step sounded behind us, and I turned to see a third European. He offered a cordial but hasty hand, and passed on ahead, shouldering a heavy staff. Halting as we halted, and moving when we moved, he kept his distance; and ever and anon tufts of herbage caught his eye, and, with curses in French, Italian, or Arabic, or all three tongues at once, he battered them furiously with the staff. I turned wondering towards Jules, who whispered, "Serpents!" Few tufts escaped, and while I walked about the Mound, this Patrick was accounting for reptiles innumerable; but alas! they lived again hydra-like as fast as he slew.

The whole *tell* was seen in half an hour. It was quite featureless, rotten with salt and of no promise to a digger. Granite blocks crumbled to shingle, and brick walls to powder at a touch. The aspect of the site was as melancholy as all the landscape about it—as the sour grey herbage, the brackish flood-waters, and the plough-lands relapsed to waste. No creak of water-wheels or plash of sluices broke the evening silence; but rotting frames stood gaunt against the sky, adding surcease of sadness to the desolation of nature.

The sun was down when we returned to the farm, but no food was set out, nor to all appearance was any being made ready. But there was more than enough *raki*. Victor made merriment for the party. He had cost in his time 30,000 francs to the Egyptian Government—moneys paid for his higher education at Paris in the glorious days of Ismail. "There you are!" cried Jules. "There's 30,000 francs—a bargain!" and the failure seemed to enjoy the inexhaustible jest as much as anyone else. I began to glean something of the past of the queer crew. The four—for yet another lurked in the house, invisible and suffering, they said, from *coup de soleil*—seemed to have held posts of profit, if not honour, on Khedivial backstairs. The farm had come to Jules from his father; but there was a long tale of water-wars with neighbouring owners and trouble with the Bedawis, of mortgages, encroachments, domiciliary visits from irrigation officials, and difficulties with tax-gatherers—all these being main incidents in the history of the surrender of three parts of the land to water and salt. The fourth part was let out to Bedawis, on whose camels or buffaloes violent hands had to be laid whenever any rent was due. The dykes and bridges had gone the way of the farmhouse, and the day seemed near when barbarism would resume an undisputed sway.

Raki is, if anything, an appetiser, and always a most unsatisfactory substitute for supper; but as the latter was not forthcoming, I was obliged to ask when and by what the pangs of hunger were to be stayed. Jules was astonished that he had not thought of supper earlier, but what could he do? Victor was cook, and Victor, it was not to be denied, was drunk. I called up my own servant, and told him to cook what he could find. Jules pronounced the idea original and admirable, and sup we did at last on potatoes and milk and bread and a tin or so of conserves from my saddle-bags. Vague associations of the past made Victor clutch now and then at my fork and spoon, only to forget them again and return to nature's tools. With *raki* once more on the board, I waived ceremony, and sought upstairs the sleep in which two of the party were sunk already where they sat. But it was long in coming. Like a traveller in an eighteenth century inn, I had better say I 'lay' that night with myriads of companions as sleepless as myself. But at some late hour I did lose consciousness only to regain it as the level beams of the sun shot through the open window. The first object of my waking vision was the unkempt Victor, whose lying down and uprising evidently were carried out with as little ceremony as his dog's. He sat with an eye to a battered telescope, and in reply to my salutation murmured an apology for being in the room, but did not avert his gaze.

Little loth to leave the bed, I stood behind him and tried to discover what he spied; but nothing did my field-glass show, except swamp and sand. Begging a sight at his spyhole, I saw more clearly the same sand and swamp, with here and there a ditch—land, once drained and probably cultivated, now glistening salt and wet in the early sun—but no stock, not even a grazing camel, and no human life. Evidently Victor had watched his labourers from afar in better days, and now could not pass his fuddled hours otherwise than by gazing where the labourers had been. It was a cheerless spectacle in the first glory of morning—that ragged figure in an unswept room with cobwebbed walls, spying phantom harvests on a salt-marsh, and the ghosts of departed hinds.

The succeeding day proved less irksome, for I spent it mostly in the sun and air, riding to various mounds, large and small. Returning at sunset, I found all as the night before, and I suppose, day in and day out, Victor sits still at his spyglass, or sleeps off *raki* upstairs; the Serpent-slayer fights his elusive foes; and the Invisible Man remains invisible. At the dawn of the third day Jules embraced me: the man with the staff went before, beating the bushes to the boundary of the farm: and Victor, who had pledged himself, as one granting a dying man's request, to keep the telescope trained upon us, till we should dip below the horizon, no doubt kept his word.

We rode back to Alexandria in one long day by a rarely travelled track round the western end of the Mariut lagoon. It is the road by which Napoleon's legions, marching on Damanhur, nearly perished of thirst; but we were to fall into no such peril, for, as the afternoon wore on, rain came up from the sea and soaked the very bones of us. Through the mist of driving storm I could see little of the desolate land, which used to be set so thick with the Mareotic vines, and nothing of the lake, except turbid wavelets chasing each other to the shallow marge. The dour Arabs of the district, who have often given trouble, had all gone to ground, and we hardly passed a house, except one or two outposts of the Slavery Prevention Service. Slithering and stumbling, the horses climbed at sunset on to the Mariut causeway, and it was the third hour of night

AN OLD FEN VILLAGE.

Facing p. 99.

before we sighted the flares in the noisome bazars of Gabbári.

I went back for the last time to the Delta some eighteen months after I had done with Crete, wishing to visit the most remote part of it, that stretch of fen and lagoon which divides Nile from Nile along the Mediterranean seaboard. This is a region apart from the rest of Egypt, and difficult to penetrate even by boat. More than the half is inundated by stagnant waters of the great river, which is dammed by a broad belt of dunes, and the land is fouled by the drainage of salt soils and by the inflowing sea. Along the shore-line itself lies an almost continuous chain of great lagoons; and for a long day's journey south of these the land will still be found deep marsh, rotten with the overflow of forgotten canals and lost arms of Nile, almost trackless, and only beginning to undergo here and there the first process of reclamation.

In their present state, as might be expected, these fens have very few inhabitants; and perhaps none of the sparse hamlets, now found on the southern fringe, is much older than the nineteenth century. Such as these are, they seem to have grown up round lonely farmsteads, and still bear the names of gentry, who, not above a generation or two ago, were living far to southward. When the Egyptian people numbered not half its present strength, under the rule of the last Mameluke Beys, there was no reason to attempt the conquest of saline and water-logged soils; and tradition remembers a not distant day—not more distant than Mehemet Ali's reign—when these fens still offered a sure, if uncomfortable, refuge to broken men who would escape the Pasha's levies, or had deserted from the battalions that were ever being sent to die in Arabia, the Sudan or Syria. The repute of the northern marshes remained indeed what it had been in the fifth century after Christ, when Heliodorus, in the opening scene of his *Aethiopic Romance*, described an amphibious outlawed folk living there by fishing and raiding. For persecuted Christians at least the marshes were a safer refuge even than the Desert: and the lone convent of Gemiana was an Egyptian Ely. I saw a poor Moslem woman bowing and muttering before the icon of Our Lady in its church, and asked what she did there. "They all come," said the monk with a shrug. "Why should she not? Her son is sick."

To some memory of this old order of things must be due the timid and surly manner which even now the inhabitants of the few older hamlets maintain. Here alone in modern Egypt *fellâhi* women will bar their doors at sight of a stranger, while the children run to hide among the reeds or scrub. Even grown men, met in the way, hold aloof like Bedawis, till assured of your character and purpose. Although the wild boar is certainly not to be found there now, many natives assert that they have seen it in past years; and twice I have come on stories even of the hippopotamus, stories told by men too savage to have learned them from foreign mouths. And why should they not have the fact from their fathers? There is good warrant for a hippopotamus having been killed in the Northern Delta in 1818.

To visit this region you quit the Berari train, which crosses mid-Delta from Dessuk on the one Nile to Sherbin on the other, at any of its halts, but best at

THE LONE CONVENT OF GEMIANA.

Facing p. 100.

Kafr es-Sheikh or Belkas; for thence roads have been made northward towards the limit of settled life. This is soon reached except along the banks of the old Nile arms, where clusters of huts succeed each other till almost within sight of the Lagoons. These tiny hamlets are built of mud into such fantastic pepper-pot forms as will throw off the frequent rains, and, seen afar, seem the work of gigantic building insects. Thereafter nothing appears ahead but the great saline flats, and vision is limited only by the curve of the globe. The monotonous surface is varied by many pools, which shrink slowly as the spring advances, leaving broad plains cracked like a crocodile's hide, and always treacherous where seeming dry; for under the thin crusts, white with efflorescent salts, lie depths of black saturated sand. Elsewhere the level is broken by soapy sand-hummocks, heaped upon shrubs or clumps of reeds, slough succeeds to slough, and the going for many miles is worse, at the best, than on loose chalk-land at the breaking of a long frost. There broods a sense of death over all this spongy salt tract, which melts into water under your heel. Nothing breaks the spell—not the many birds shocking in their tameness; not the myriad mosquitoes which pursue a traveller luckless enough to ride down wind; not the teeming life of the ditches; not the half-wild buffaloes, strayed from southern farmsteads, which you startle from their wallows, and send soughing knee-deep through the slime; not even the tireless north wind which lashes the huddled reeds. Yet with all its sameness and deadness one likes the land. The breeze blows hard and clear off sea and lagoon—hard and clear, as through the bolt ropes about a mast—, and the flats have the mysterious charm of all large and free horizons.

To the soapy bogs and salt lagoons fall drains and canals, which have sprung far up the Delta to die at last unregarded under the face of the dunes; and there is also a network of forgotten waterways of Ptolemaic and Roman days which now wander unguided. A day will often be half spent in seeking a ford from one of their crumbling banks to the other. Sometimes you must strip under a noonday sun among the ever wakeful mosquitoes; at other times, but rarely, you may be ferried in the log-boat of a marshman, son of former outlaws, who spends his days afishing and his nights prone under just such a bee-hive shelter of reeds and mud as a lake-dweller built in the age of stone. Heliodorus, who wrote of boats "rudely hewed out of the rough tree," which crept about these channels in 400 A.D., saw the fenland much as it all was till lately and as it still is in the remote parts of Menzaleh. Thus he wrote as Underdowne rendered him.

The whole place is called the Pasture of the Egyptians, about the which is a lowe valley, which receiveth certaine exundations of Nylus, by means whereof it becometh a poole, and is in the midst very deepe, about the brimmes whereof are marishes or fennes. For looke, as the shore is to the Sea, such is the Fennes to every great Poole. In that place have the theeves of Egypt, how many soever they bee, their common wealth. And for as much as there is a little land without the water, some live in small cottages, others in boates which they use as wel for their house as for passage over the poole. In these doe their women serve them, and if need require, be also brought to bedde. When a child is borne first, they let him suck his mother's milk a while, but after they feede him with fishes taken in the lake and roasted in the hot sunne. And when they perceive that he beginnes to goe, they tie a cord about his legs, and suffer him but onely to goe about the

A FEN FISHERMAN.

Facing p. 102.

boate. . . . Moreover the great plenty of reede that groweth there in the moozy ground is in a manner as good as a bulwark to them. For by devising many crooked and cumbrous wayes, through which the passage to *them* by oft use is very easie, but to *others* hard, they have made it as a sure defence, that by no sudden invasion they may be endammaged.

Yet once there were towns in this sodden land, which raised not only corn to stay the hunger of Rome, but vines and olives. Some two score mounds, covering as many towns, rise out of the maze of irrigation channels and choked drains, and you may see still the bed-stones of oil-presses and faint traces of ridge and furrow on higher lying patches. It is a mystery how men ever lived and tilled in a land, whither one would surely say

no man comes
Nor hath come since the making of the world.

For they had no pumps, those husbandmen of the Roman time, and their drainage must have been by natural flow. Has all the Delta sunk slowly since their day, even as its shore has plainly been sinking at Alexandria ever since those Ptolemaic buildings, which are now awash in the eastern bay, were built high and dry on Lechaeum?

Even on the margin of the great northern lagoons, where Heliodorus' *ichthyophagi* still survive, you can ride nowhere far without happening on ancient tracks of civilised man. Basins hollowed for flat-bottomed shipping, and silted canals with broken dykes, mock again and again your sanguine essay of a bee-line to some far seen Tell. Arrived at last, after many a false turn and lure of cheating mirage, you will find no imposing ruin; for in this region builders used little except brick, and the most of it adobe. But the surface will be seen strewn with vitreous slags, left by Arabs, who have burnt what stone there was for lime; with fragments of iridescent glass, that vies with the green hues of copper scraps and coins; with sherds of crumbling blue faience and red earthenware. It is meagre loot after so much toil through bog and soapy sand; nor is much more to be got by digging at a venture. The mounds are made mostly of little adobe houses, piled one on another, and rotted through and through with salt; and below these, if you are hopeful enough to dig, you will pass through some feet of empty sand, compressed to the consistency of asphalt, only to find at the bottom a core of black Nile mud, heaped by the first builders to raise their town above the damp of the surrounding flats. Now and again the newly come natives, who dig in these mounds for the nitrous earth, which exists on all ancient sites by the Nile, or for ready-made bricks, have turned up drums or capitals of small columns, an inscription or two, or even a Roman sculpture—trophies all of an Empire, under whose rule Egypt was more widely tilled than even at this day. But these are rare rewards.

The lagoons lie farther yet, and, if you would see them well, you must sail before the summer heats down one of the greater canals of the Delta in a boat of the lightest draught. The last lock is left far behind, and you pass beyond all hamlets into an amphibious Limbo where no life of man abides. The canal has no longer dykes on either hand, and its rims sink below your gunwale. Drop down a mile or two more. The flood brims bank high, and slops on to the flats, and, before you are

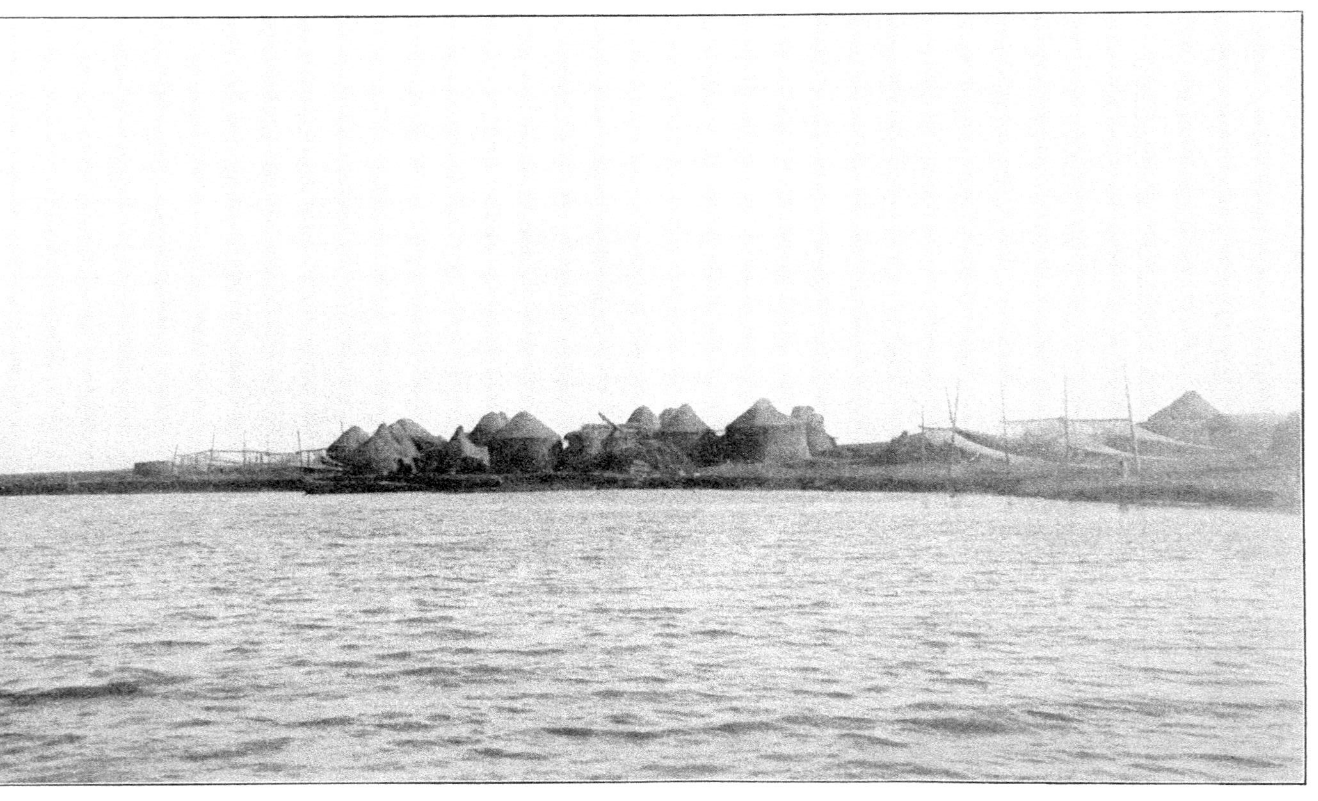

THE NORTHERNMOST HAMLET.

Facing p. 105.

well aware, the Nile land has slid under its own waters. You are out on a Lagoon, boundless and bottomless to all appearance, so low are its shores, and so turbid its harassed waves. Yet, in fact, when a tall man lets himself down in mid-lake, the ripples hardly wash his breast.

Holding on your course, you find that you have passed out of the dead world of the fens into one of teeming life. Of this the aspect of the northernmost hamlet on the canal may have forewarned you, for scores of fishing nets were spread there to wind and sun, beside a little fleet of keelless craft, and a Copt was selling to all comers the last night's draught of fish. The catch of each crew is offered in gross. A salesman, squatting on a mat, stirs the throbbing pile, working the larger fish to the top. A fat one he puts by in a palm-leaf pannier for the Copt, a second for his writer, a third for himself, and the residue is bid for at ten, twenty, forty piastres, sold, packed on asses, and driven off to be marshmen's food for many miles around. The fishy wealth of the Lagoon is amazing. Silvery shapes leap in air by tens and twenties, and passing shoals leave wakes in every direction. Boats at anchor, boats adrift, boats under full sail, multiply as one runs northward; and out of the horizon spring groves of poles crossed by poles aslant, masts and yards of invisible hulls moored by invisible islets, whose sandy levels are all but awash. There must be hundreds of craft plying on Lake Burullos, and its fisher-folk are legion—men of blond colouring, active and somewhat silent, with the refined facial type common to old inbred races. Their women often recalled to me pictures that I had seen on the Pharaonic monuments.

The farther shore does not begin to rise on the north-eastern horizon till a dozen barren islets have slipped astern. The higher dunes emerge first, uplifted in a shimmering mirage, roseate and yellow like cumulus lit by sunset. One into another they run, till they become a continuous range, spotted with black tufts, which are the plumes of half-buried palms. A cluster of huts to the left, with square upstanding blocks, is the village of Borg, whose dismantled fort and coastguard station mark the shrunken Sebennytic estuary of Nile. Rank odours of curing come down the wind from its drying grounds which supply half the poor of Lower Egypt. On the starboard bow, as you wear round the last island and set a course due east, a large dark stain resolves itself into a little town distinguished by a minaret or two, which is set on a hillock backed by golden dunes and palms. A forest of naked masts and yards bristles on the lake before it—the fleet of Baltim, chief settlement of the fisher-folk, and the old see, Parallos.

The lake floor here has so slight a slope that a mile from its marge the water is still only inches deep, and the grounded feluccas must discharge their freights on to camels, which are trained against nature to receive their loads standing and wade unconcerned to the shore. Naked children splash all day in the shoal-water, plying tiny javelins and little casting-nets, so far out as to seem no bigger than gulls; and there could be no healthier or happier babes than this amphibious brood, whose playground is the Lagoon. Their fathers and mothers seem to pass the day on the vast stretch of sandy beach, coopering boats, buying and selling fish, chattering, sleeping in the sun. It is astonishing to see so clean a life in Egypt, a life unfouled by the viscous

CAMELS LOADING AT BALTIM.

Facing p. 106.

HALF BURIED PALM-FOREST, BALTIM.

Facing p. 107.

ink of the Nile mud. Even the huts are not built of clay, but of ancient Roman bricks dug out of mounds south of the Lagoon, and long ago mellowed to a dusky red that tones to admiration with the yellow dunes and the dark greenery of the palms. Bee-hive shelters, byres and fences are wattled of dry palm-fronds.

Coming out of the great southern flats to this long sand-belt, which fences the northern sea, one has an illusion of upland, and, climbing over the sliding dunes, credits with difficulty that the land falls to the Nile level in every deeper hollow. Here palms, planted deep, are bearing abundantly, though the dunes in their constant eastward progression bury them to the spring of their plumes. Potatoes, too, and tomatoes are grown behind long alignments of sheltering wattles; nor even on the dunes is there lacking a wild, waxy pasture whose roots trail fifty or sixty feet to find a moister soil. A region not dissimilar may be seen from the Rosetta railway, and Edku, by its lake, is a village somewhat like Baltim. But there is no view west of the Nile to rival that from the higher dunes of Baltim; nothing like its forest of sand-choked palms stretched ribandwise between the low lake-dunes and the golden sea-ward hillocks; nothing like the ample prospect of its lake, fringed with fisher hamlets, alive with splashing children, and bearing a distant burden of myriad amber sails.

CHAPTER V.

THE SATALIAN GULF.

IN the early spring of 1904 the owner of the beautiful yacht, Utowana, invited me to a cruise in Levant waters. We coasted Crete, revisiting familiar spots, and then headed for Anatolia, where the long Carian fiords offer perfect shelter and much of present beauty and former fame, which you may not see easily except from a private ship. Didymi and Iassus, Bargylia and Budrum, Cnidus, Loryma, Rhodes and the Lycian cities, which I had visited seven years before, drew us to land day after day, and it was full April when we made Cape Chelidonia, and bore up into the Satalian Gulf.

The sky had cleared after some days of south-westerly weather, and morning broke in that rare splendour which persuaded the Hebrew poets, that perfect bliss will be perfect light. A long creaming swell heaved like opalescent satin, set with dusky pearls of islets; and the Norse deck-hands vented their joy of life in signalling ecstatically to the astonished crew of a caique, which was rocking on the fairy sea. The lust of movement grew in us also till we found the yacht too small. Where could we go ashore on that lovely land? One bethought him of the famous undying fire of Chimaera which few have seen in the Lycian forest,

THE UTOWANA AT CNIDUS.

Facing p. 108.

and begged that we might put into Deliklitash and range afield. The Owner was willing; a new course was set, and we slanted towards the shore.

For an hour we hugged the crags, then, as a broad bay opened below wooded steeps, wore round till the glittering pyramid of Takhtaly was on our starboard bow. A shelving bank of shingle appeared ahead, and behind it, a narrow ribbon of fields and garden grounds, divided by a stream, which issued from a black cleft in the horse-shoe of cliffs. Half a dozen roofs peeped out of the trees, and presently, as a red ensign shook itself out on the single flagstaff to welcome the rare visit of what was thought a ship of war, we descried a little knot of eager figures gathering to the beach. Anchor was dropped far out (for soundings were none too frequent on the charts), and the whale-boat's men had to pull long and strong before our bow grated on the shingle, and was hauled high and dry by willing hands. The Stars and Stripes had probably never flown before off Deliklitash. Our latest predecessor seems to have been the Crown Prince of Italy, now King, who called some years ago, and left a pleasant memory, which went for something in our reception. At any rate all ashore seemed glad of our coming, and emulously offered guidance to *Yanár*, the Fire, assuming without further question that, like our royal forerunner, we were come to see Chimaera.

The path led northward at first, across the shallow stream, into gardens where we threaded our way among irrigation ditches, in defiance of protesting hounds, and through and under a various vegetation rioting for room. The little plain, which faces south-east below gigantic firebricks of red rock, must grill in summer noons in the climate of a hot-house; and even on an April morning, after a spell of storm, it seemed a valley where snow could never come nor any wind blow coldly. Certainly none was blowing then, and our gait of emulous exhilaration sobered gradually as the sun rose higher, and the path sloped upwards over the short turf of a ravine where camels were browsing. Once through the gardens, we were to see no human being except a herd-boy, feeding his kine near the sea, and little sign of the hand or foot of man. The forest straggled to meet us in clumps of holm-oak and plane on the floor of the ravine, but spread a thicker mantle of pine and fir up the steepening slopes, till checked by cornices of angry volcanic crag. It is not often that one walks in Turkey so free of police or fear of land-lopers, among unfamiliar flowers and birds and butterflies. The guide talked of the chase as a Lycian farmer, sportsman in grain, will always talk, telling tales of bears which come down into the little plain to forage on winter nights; of boars which rout in the garden grounds; of myriad partridges and francolins, of which, however, we saw and shot but one; of leopards, and also of lions, which he believed might yet be found in the wilder hills. No European has ever shot in Lycia, or so much as seen, alive or dead, the royal beast whose effigy is so often carved on Lycian tombs; and maybe, this *arslán* of Deliklitash was no more than the panther, which ranges other Anatolian mountains, less unknown than the Lycian Alps.

Arrived abreast of a ruddy patch on the northern side of the ravine, which he said was the dump-heap of an ancient copper mine, the guide bore away to the left, and led us up the steep slope among pines.

There was no track but such as goats make, and the rock-steps made long striding for booted and gaitered men; but our Lycian, who was shod with close-bound layers of hide and wool, the most suitable gear in the world for rocks, light as a mocassin and pliable as a sock, bounded up them like his goats. Some of us would not be beaten by him; others frankly refused to keep his pace; and in very open order we came up at last, breathless and crimson, into a little dell, about a thousand feet above the ravine, bare of trees, and floored with an ashen crust. A huddle of mean ruins lay in the desolate clearing, which looked like the tailing of a furnace, and smelt of leaking coal gas. "*Ishté*"! said the guide, "There you are! YANÁR!"

What disillusion! Where were those eternal fires of Chimaera? The sun beat pitilessly on the little hollow, which seemed burned out, blanched, dead. Was this what we had come up to see? The last arrived of us, the least cool and most disgusted, made a bee-line for the ruins, cried out, and jumped aside. We followed with more wariness, and, behold, the Fire was at our feet. Tongues of flame, spirituous, colourless, well nigh invisible in that white glare, were licking the mouths of a dozen vents—flames inextinguishable, inexhaustible, fed by nothing seen or felt. The guide said other fires would break out wherever water was poured, and drawing from a mountain rivulet hard by, we found it so. The largest vent opens almost beneath the main group of ruin, which has evidently once been a church, raised with the stones of some older building. A Greek inscription is encrusted in the blistered wall, and surely some pagan temple has stood here to the Spirit of the Fire. On the edge of the clearing, half hidden in thorn scrub, rise ruins of another building of many chambers, to whose crumbling walls mouldering frescoes of saints still cling. Here, doubtless, dwelt the monks who served the church. Trees and bushes on all hands were hung with rags, vicarious vouchers for former wearers. That was all. A second patch like this and similar ruins, said the guide, were to be found higher up the mountain; but we did not go to the place, and thus saw no more of Chimaera than that half-acre of pallid slag, with its lambent elusive flames, scorched ruins, and beggarly memorials of modern pagans rotting on leafless boughs.

Nevertheless, when we turned to go down the hill we were well content. We had found no wonder, for, except by night, when the burning patch is a far-seen beacon at sea, the spectacle is no great matter. But we had been on holy ground, where man has communed with the Earth Spirit since first he broke into the Lycian wilds. Those piacular rags, those temple stones, bore sufficient witness that so he believed and still believes. There is no record of the name by which he called the Spirit; but in all likelihood, when Christianity had won him, he raised his church here to the Panaghía, the All Holy, the Virgin Mother, whose honour nine out of ten churches in Western Asia Minor commemorate. There are many Christian shrines, of course, in the Nearer East which bear other names than hers, dedicated to obscure saints who never lived; and there are tombs enough, honoured as resting-places of other saints who never died, cenotaphs as vain as those barrows which are supposed by Islamic piety to cover in double and triple the giant bones of Patriarchs drowned in the

PHASELIS AND TAKHTALY.

Facing p. 113.

Flood, or as the *turbé's* of early Moslem champions, who, in fact, died decently in far Arabian oases, or were eaten of birds and dogs in passes of Syria. But most of these shrines and tombs are peculiar sanctuaries, holy places of particular tribal groups, whose ghostly tenants passed through many metempsychoses, before they found their final peace as Saint This or Abu That; whereas the Panaghía enjoys universal honour in all this region, having inherited from the one great Nature Goddess, who was worshipped of old under so many names—Leto and Artemis, Kybele and Mylitta, Baalit and Ashtoreth, and others still earlier, which are not known to us.

Anchor was up by early afternoon, and we dropped down the coast northwards to Tekir Ova, once Phaselis, the most easterly city which paid the Athenian tribute. Right over us hung a mountain whose eight thousand feet rise from the sea-line to the snow. Takhtaly is the proudest peak on the exquisite Anatolian coast, perhaps on any coast at all of the Mediterranean sea, and, seen from south, east, or north, will be remembered when many a loftier mountain has been forgotten. It is the great glory of Phaselis; but even were it away, the site of the city would be one of the most beautiful in the Greek lands, whether for its prospect over the purple gulf to the Tauric Alps, or for its nearer setting. The main group of habitations lay on a peninsula of jutting rock, which falls sheer to the sea on three sides, and probably was once an island, though not in historic times; for an ancient aqueduct straddles the sandy isthmus. The lie of the land gave the city two harbours, of which the southern is large, shallow, and silted up, while the northern is the most pellucid rock-bay imaginable, still fringed with broken quays and fenced by a broken mole. All eastern Lycia is now become wilderness; but Tekir Ova is a wilder spot than most. The site seems to have been little worth anyone's while to quarry, and the Greek, Roman, and Byzantine ruins have been left for Nature to appropriate as best she may. On the high part of the peninsula the sturdy cistus shrubs, which have found root in every corner and cranny, have helped wind and weather to break down the buildings bit by bit into such vast hummocks as a terrific earthquake might leave; and sprouting thickest in all hollows, the thorns, which fence each great heap, let no man through without taking toll of his garments and skin. The main street, flanked by the theatre and other public buildings, which ran across the isthmus from one harbour to the other, is now become one long grove of evergreen and deciduous trees, which have thrust down many a wall, and trail their fingers over carved and inscribed stones; and the fortuitous avenue frames some very pretty effects, the best being a glimpse of the northern harbour, seen in vignette down a green tunnel. But none of human kind passes to and fro in this street any more. Fauns and hamadryads are all you will see in the longest vigil.

There is no monument worth a pilgrimage. The theatre is small and collapsed; the temples are buried beneath their own ruin, and become shaggy hillocks; the buildings about the market place are choked, and hardly more visible in the brake than the Castle in the Sleeping Wood. A file of white marble gravestones, which lines the northward road, alone makes a show. But it is worth going all the way to Phaselis to see only the gracious revenge which Nature takes on those who were once her lords.

Tekir Ova is a type of what one may see so often along these coasts of Asia Minor—at every few miles an ancient seaport, its moles abandoned to the waves and its streets to the fox and the jackal. The busy modern centres of life in Asia Minor lie out of sight of the sea, the few exceptions being towns whose spring of life resides in an alien people, and not in the masters of the land. The Turk is in fault, of course, both because he ever withdraws his land, like his house, from the sight of alien men, and also because, in his distaste of the sea, he formerly allowed corsairs to scare the villages into the hills. But if that fault has been his, a like fault was committed also by others long before him. Not only are modern settlements lacking on the Anatolian shores, but, it seems, very ancient ones as well. The coastal sites have yet to show evidence of primaeval times, and all the native Anatolian cities of the remoter age, thus far known, except Hissarlik, lie inland, and the traces of the earliest civilisation have been found out of sight of the sea. Ephesus has yielded no prehistoric things, nor have any Ionian or Carian sites, which have been explored, given us more. The Turk has but done what all eastern rulers of Asia Minor, from the Hittite to the Persian, did before him.

At Phaselis we saw the last of Lycia, except her higher snows, which open out, peak behind peak, in the backward view from the northern shore of the Gulf ; and we passed on to Pamphylia, the land of All Tribes in antiquity and still a home for the scrapings and leavings of peoples. Whenever the Ottoman Government wants place for refugees, it plants them in Pamphylia. Thither have come Moslems from Greece during the war of independence, and Moslems from Crete since the Liberation; Circassians and Bulgars, at any time during the past generation; and gypsies at all times since the Ottoman conquest. All alike live as though halting for no more than the day, and waiting the word to go farther and fare better—or worse. There are very few villages, and those that exist seem not of the country. Even as progress is reckoned in Asiatic Turkey, Pamphylia is an unprogressive land, where no one appears to think it worth his while to do more than mark time. Why residence there should be so little desired, I know not. Perhaps it is undesirable. With their southward aspect, and great mountain screen to the north, the coastal plains must be intensely hot in the summer months; and since they are largely alluvial and in many parts marshy, mosquitoes and fever are probably all too rife. But just because it is so desolate now, Pamphylia keeps the most wonderful memorials of her past. Termessus and Perga, Aspendus and Sidé were not very great or famous cities in their day, and were it not for Paul the Apostle, had hardly been known by name to the modern world at large. But their remote ruins have survived as have hardly any others of their epoch, and all are famous cities now.

About the third hour of the day we were off the mouth of the Eurymedon river, cruising above the Persian wrecks, which were sunk by Cimon the Athenian. Balkis Kalé—for Aspendus has so appealed to oriental imagination as to be renamed, with other magic "castles," after Solomon's Arabian Queen—lies some miles up stream, and the Owner proposed, if his petrol launch could pass the bar, to take us by water to the site. The deep discolour of the sea a mile offshore warned us that the river was running high, and a Greek fisherman, brought from Adalia to be pilot, prophesied we should pass easily into the mouth, but soon meet too fierce a current. He was to prove right; but for awhile we discredited him, finding not only water enough and to spare on the bar, but the launch making easy way up a placid flood, which glided almost bank high between earthy flats, not unlike the lower Delta lands of Egypt in vegetation and colour. There seemed at first few men or beasts on either hand, and such as there were stared astonished beyond measure at sight of a bark breasting the stream without oar or sail or smoke. But soon a large village of Cretan refugees rose into view on a mound some distance from the right bank, and as the channel curved eastward, two caiques at anchor appeared ahead. Pointing to them our pilot said we could float so far but no farther, and before we were well abreast of them he was justified. The current, which had run thus far three miles an hour against the launch, quickened to five and six, and our keel began to touch ground from one moment to another. There was nothing for it but to make fast, walk to the nearest hamlet, and seek horses.

These proved hard to find. There were few houses, and those widely spaced among fields and gardens. Most had but a single upper chamber built over a cow-byre (as men build in marshy plains), and half were empty and locked. The rest sheltered rather taciturn peasants, who seemed to live lonely lives, each man for himself. None bade us welcome, and none, till forced by the men of our escort, would fetch his beast from pasture and take a double hire. It was near noon, therefore, before we were mounted and away, and even by hustling unwilling horses, we could hope for no more than a very short stay at Balkís. The path ran among untilled hillocks, and now and again opened a view of some foaming reach of the river. So long as we kept the left bank, there was little to look at except the same Tauric snows which had closed our northward view for a week past. At one point we passed out of the scrub into a grassy clearing dappled with the shadows of old cedars, where half a dozen brood mares pastured, each with her foal, under the sole guard of four huge dogs; but even there no man appeared, nor were we to see one till we struck the river again at its single bridge, a decayed and dangerous relic of a better age, built bowwise to meet the stream. Here on the right bank stood a caravanserai, whence a knot of gypsies ran out to stare as we crossed. Their winter camp lay beside our farther road, a huddle of black tents and bamboo huts, of yapping puppy-dogs, squalling babies, elfin women and sooty kettles, among which we drew rein to gaze a moment on the distant bulk of the Theatre of Aspendus—to gaze from the ephemeral dwellings of a society which defies Time towards the imperishable monument of a society which Time has long ago destroyed.

You may have seen amphitheatres in Italy, France, Dalmatia and Africa; temples in Egypt and Greece; palaces in Crete; you may be sated with antiquity, or scornful of it. But you have not seen the Theatre of Aspendus. It has at once the grandeur of scale which excites fancy, and that perfection in survival which, lulling the sense of strangeness, allows fancy to leap unastonished across

THE THEATRE OF ASPENDUS.

Facing p. 118.

IN THE THEATRE OF ASPENDUS.

Facing p. 119.

the centuries. In every other Roman theatre, which I have seen, some part of the *cavea* is perished, the uppermost tiers at any rate being merged so irregularly into the hillside that one may hardly know where seats end and naked rock begins; or else jungle intrudes on the auditorium, and the *scena* wall, even if so perfect as at Orange, stands a dreary skeleton, with not only its marble statues lost, but all marble mouldings and casing whatsoever. Thus, whether one look up or down, all illusion that the building might still serve its first purpose, is cheated. But at Aspendus, not only is every bench in its place and perfect, but the *cavea* is still crowned with the original arcade which served as a finish and coping to the whole. Vegetation has hardly been able to take root in the close joints of the masonry, and the ancient drains and gutters, which are still serviceable, have suffered little silt to settle in the orchestra. From the stage buildings little is missing, and from the scena wall nothing, except the contents of the niches. All stones are still square and sharp, and the courses are true as if laid yesterday. The whole building, moreover, is of gigantic size, erected not at divers epochs by the city, but all at once by the pious munificence of one wealthy individual, desirous to outdo all other citizens of the Empire in gratitude for the victorious return of Lucius Verus from the East; and under the inscription by which this his act is recorded for all time to come, one enters the main portal to right of the stage. A taciturn officer of the Adalia police, who had ridden up with us, stood stock still a moment under this great doorway, and then went off by himself, looking curiously at every part of the corridors, stage and seats. At last he came back, accepted a cigarette, and stared slowly round the great horseshoe. "What sort of men," he asked, "were here before us? No Osmanli built this."

Taken all in all, the Theatre of Aspendus is perhaps the most splendid of all the great Roman buildings that time has spared. Certainly it is the first and greatest of the surviving theatres, and the one which fancy may most easily repeople with its ancient audience and dead players. You can imagine yourself strayed into it on an off-day, and look for the slaves to come and set it in order for a performance on the morrow; and, as in the Temple of Edfu, you tread softly, as a stranger doubtful of his right of entry.

It is hard to leave this Theatre; but when you do, follow the line of the city wall up to the table-land behind, where was the market-place, not to see only its ruined porticoes nor yet the shell of a great Basilica, which rises out of the brushwood, nor yet again the two marble statues lying near it, which perhaps were passed over by Verres when he robbed Aspendus to enrich his gallery; but to see also the northward view. The site lies on the rocky roots of Taurus, just where the Eurymedon escapes from a gorge whose fringing scarps lead the eye step by step into the farthest blue of the hills. The mountain screen, which shuts off the central Anatolian lakes, is more boldly carved into peak and buttress behind Aspendus than I have seen it elsewhere, and is more nobly wooded to the verge of the spring snows. Few palaces have so fair a prospect as the Castle of Queen Balkís.

The next morning found the Utowana a few miles further east, at Old Adalia, settled, within the last year

TURKS IN THE CORRIDOR AT ASPENDUS.

Facing p. 120.

THE THEATRE OF SIDÉ.

Facing p. 121.

or two, by some two hundred Cretan families, who have made themselves dwellings within the shell of Sidé. Here is the wreck of a theatre only less enormous than that at Aspendus. Since there was no convenient hill-side to be hollowed, the auditorium has been raised on arches like a half Coliseum, and it survives almost whole; but the scena wall has collapsed upon the stage in a mighty cataract of stones. One part of the ancient city is still a labyrinth of ruin; the other has been cleared and built upon by the Cretans. The exiles seemed ill at ease in their refuge. The Sultan had given them land and houses; but their fields, they said, were stony, and they lacked cattle for the plough; the water was bad, and they found they could talk little with their Greek tongues to the surrounding folk. It was hard, they thought, to have to begin life afresh, and for what fault? None the less, they seemed to be setting brave faces towards the future, and making the best of their fortune; and though they knew well enough that men of English speech had weighted the scale against their creed in Crete, they showed no rancour towards us, but were glad to trade in ancient coins and scarcely younger eggs. They bethought them, too, of other antiques in marble and terra-cotta, which they had found while collecting stones from Sidé, or turning its soil with their spades; and in the event, we spent some exhilarating hours in unashamed quest of forbidden things.

It were easy enough now to justify our looting, for, else, those marbles had gone long ago into the limekiln. But I doubt if any one of us thought a moment about justification, as we were loading the whale-boat once and again with spoils of Sidé. We were filled full of the lust of loot, possessing ourselves of treasure ready-made, reaping that we had not sown, tasting a joy which recks as little of justification as any on earth. It is the joy which has made pirates and filibusters and mercenary adventurers of all sorts and conditions of men, and kept them so till death. It recruited Greeks to fight for Persia, and Germans to fight for Rome, Norsemen to fight for Constantinople, and anyone and everyone to fight in Grand Companies, and Knightly Orders, and Janissary and Mameluke battalions; and it will recruit their like to the end of time. It has no rivals among motives of human action, but Love and Fear, and it has so often conquered both, that who will say, the greatest of these three is not the Lust of Loot?

CHAPTER VI.

CYRENE.

After coasting Cilicia and Cyprus for an idle week, the Utowana headed out to sea once more. We were bound for Cyrene, or so near at least as we might go to that long forbidden city. Had the party not been all of American nationality but one, we should never perhaps have put our luck to the test at all. But the Youngest Race sees no reason why it should not go anywhere on earth, and so it came about that the Utowana made the African shore late on a misty afternoon, and anchored off Ras el-Tin.

Under a red bar of sunset, Cyrenaica looked a grim land. Shelving up in low desert planes, treeless, houseless, tentless, it put us in mind more of present danger from Bedawi landlopers and Senussi fanatics than of the past glory of Cyrene. The latest news of the inner country, which had been current in Europe, reported it closed to Christians by a Government conscious that it could not guarantee them against the Senussi Order, which it was unwilling to offend. This mysterious Brotherhood was a bugbear of which we, like most people, knew very little. Widely spread and greatly respected through all north Africa, powerful in Mecca, and at one time, at any rate, not less powerful in Stambul, it had long been credited with a fanatic hatred of Christians, and indeed of all such Moslems as will make terms with Christendom, even the Caliph himself. Two generations ago it fixed its chief seat on Jebel Akhdar in Cyrenaica, attracted by the loneliness of the well-watered highlands; and although, since 1876, its leaders have been withdrawing by stages into the heart of Africa, we knew that two score Senussi convents flourished still about Cyrene, and had drawn the local Bedawis to them. In the early eighties, when Abdul Hamid was hoping to push his Islamic policy by means of the Brotherhood, the real power in Tripolitan Turkey was given into its hands; and Duveyrier, who set himself to study its aims and work in the oases behind French Africa, charged it with the constant endeavour to stay by robbery and murder all Frank advance. Others took up his cry, and pointed in proof to the killing of the Marquis de Morés by men of Ghadámes, as he was feeling his way towards Kufra. Our latest forerunner in Cyrene had found the Bedawis still as hostile to his presence as Murdoch Smith and James Hamilton had found them to theirs; and nothing, to our knowledge, had happened since to make the outlook more hopeful.

But, in fact, a certain change of good omen had taken place, as we were to learn next day in Derna. Well received in that pleasant half-Moorish town, whose coral beach and deep palm groves make it an outpost of tropic Africa, while its clean alleys, fair gardens, and grave, well-seeming Arabs, suggest an oasis town of Nejd, we heard that Cretan colonists were newly come to Cyrenaica. A hundred refugee families, it was said, had settled at Marsa Susa, and sixty about Ain Shahát, as Arabs name the Apollo fountain at Cyrene; and beside each colony a handful of Ottoman troops was encamped. True, Christians were still forbidden to travel in the inner country; but with credentials from Derna, said the Italian who flies our flag there on high days and holidays, we might drop anchor at Marsa Susa, and ask an escort to Ain Shahát. He himself had been there lately with a friend, and had found the mudir a most liberal Turk, who would rejoice to see us. So there was a mudir? Yes, a civilian officer who was gripping the Bedawis tighter every day. And the Senussis, what of them? He replied that, with the mudir on the spot and an escort to show that the Government was for us, there would be no trouble. Indeed, in these days, he added, the convents showed no ill-will to Europeans. He took us presently to call on the Governor, a fat little Candiote of an inordinate garrulity and a tremulous anxiety to please, who gave us the needful letter on the spot and then, after his kind, repented him bitterly, and asked for it again. But we held firm and, as we rowed out again to the yacht, on a night too warm for the season, over waters which doubled every star and the full globe of the moon, our minds were easy. There was no telegraph then in Cyrenaica, and the yacht could drop down to Marsa Susa many hours ahead of any mounted messenger from Derna.

Within five hours she was anchored there off the old city of Apollonia, which is become an heap; and in two more half her passengers, with an escort of seven soldiers and our Derniote friend's *kavass* for guide, were mounted on two spavined white mares, two donkeys, and a camel. The yacht was left to rock on the treacherous roadstead outside the reefs, and the Owner, turning his back on his beautiful ship, put up a prayer that the land-wind which had followed the fair but fickle southerly breeze of the day before, might hold till the morrow. We had yet to learn that in Cyrenaica the *Khamsin* of Egypt is apt to pass into the dread *Gharbîs*, a gale veering between south-west and north, from whose wrath there is no safe shelter at Marsa Susa, or indeed anywhere else on the coast for some hundreds of miles; so we kicked up our beasts and jogged merrily inland past plots of red tillage, and feeding flocks, and Cretan shepherds leaning on old Belgian rifles, towards the foot of the scarp up which a rock road of the ancients leads to Cyrene.

Forgotten highways always seem to me haunted places: and, since even second sight can be sharpened by realities, the better preserved a highway is, the better you see its ghosts. Therefore, if you would be fey, ride alone and by night from Apollonia to Cyrene through tangled forests and across deserted glades, treading pavements which dead men have worn. This strange way in the wilderness is not heaped up like a Roman road, but chiselled squarely out of living rock. Its raised side-walks still align it on either hand, and the tracks of Greek chariots and Libyan carts are cut deep on its face. For twenty centuries it has borne its witness to the grandeur that was once Cyrene, and it will bear it still for unnumbered centuries to come.

Except for the stirring sight of it, we found our ride to Cyrene an irksome exercise. The sky was clouded with coming scirocco, the air hung heavy, and there was no water by the way for our flagging beasts or the marching escort of Syrian soldiers. But here a ruined

THE ROCK ROAD FROM APOLLONIA TO CYRENE.

Facing p. 126.

TOMBS OF CYRENE.

Facing p. 127.

fort guarding a pass, there a group of sarcophagi, and everywhere the curves and cuttings of the road fed imagination, and shortened the hours, till, at an elbow of the climbing track, we came suddenly in sight of the tombs of Cyrene. There was yet a mile to go through the suburb of the dead, and with every step our wonder grew. Fresh from the carved cliffs of Lycia, we were not prepared for a finer spectacle in Africa. Terraced from top to bottom of the mountain buttresses, the pillared rock-graves of Cyrene rise in Doric, Ionic, and hybrid styles. Yet the more splendid fronts amaze one less than the endless tiers of commoner graves, mere rock-pits with gabled lids, which are cut out by thousands, with hardly a foot's breadth between them, on the hill sides. When later on we entered a larger tomb here and there, we often found behind one narrow façade a catacomb parcelled out in niches for half a hundred dead, whose beds have been used again and again. In modern days we set our cemeteries apart within walls and in remote spots, fearing the corpse as we might a vampire, and rarely make the houses of the dead an embellishment of cities. But the Greek, and the Roman after him, who held serried graves to be the noblest civic avenue, lavished art on the last homes of hero-spirits to make them the chief glories of their towns; and Death must have lost half its sting for those who knew they would lie beside the main road in tombs seen of all wayfaring men and praised in distant lands.

Among the myriad mansions of the dead we heard the first sounds of men. Voices cried to us from tombs opening high on a hill-side below a thin crown of pines; but the two or three troglodytes, who came out to view, went back at sight of our soldiers. Unmet and unsaluted, we followed the splendid curves and counter-curves of the road, till at last it ran out on a level stretch ; and there near a single hut of rough stones, under the bloody flag of Turkey, we came on the booted mudir himself in council with four spearmen of the Haasa. He looked up in some astonishment and trouble, for few and far between are European visitors to Cyrene. But the breeding of a Turk, the custom of Islam, and the sight of our *Iradé*, secured us hospitality in his bullet-proof room, built above a Roman sepulchre.

We were not minded, however, to sit long over a mudir's coffee, and presently went forth again to see something of the city before dark fell. The scirocco had not yet veiled, though it dimmed, the distance, and we could understand, if not echo, the rapture of lucky travellers, who in clear weather have looked across the cemeteries to the cornlands of the lower plateau. The sea swelled grey to the horizon, confounded with the dun northward sky ; and in the nearer view stretched the broad belt of ruddy soil, now not half ploughed, which was once the pride of Cyrene. A green ribband, spreading fanwise as it sloped, marked the course of the Apollo waters, captured and distributed by the Senussis ; and a sinuous line of scarps and tree-tops, winding westward, was, we were told, the vaunted Wady bil-Ghadir, the Happy Valley, where are other tombs as splendid as any which we had seen. The greater monuments, such as the Theatre and the Apollo Temple itself, of which last little is visible except the platform on which the main building once stood, lie along the higher course of the Apollo stream. Southward, also, the view from

THE MUDIR OF CYRENE.

Facing p. 129

the crest of the plateau is amazing, not for ruins of the city, of which little enough stands up now out of the corn, but for the immensity of the site. Cyrene was built at the summit of a slope which falls steeply to the sea but gently inland, melting southward into steppe at the limit of vision, and for miles and miles is dotted with fragments of grey ruin. The Bedawis say that it is six camel-hours from one end to another of "Grené," as the name "Kyrene" has been softened in their mouths. No site of antiquity so well suggests how a large city of our own day will seem when at last deserted by man.

All that we saw then in fast fading light we should see better on the morrow, and it was not worth while to do more than climb the height above the Apollo Fountain, which was surely the acropolis of the city. A Cretan came out of a tomb, and showed us this and that bit of moulding or sculpture, betraying a Greek's brain below his turban; but such Bedawis as we crossed in the way saluted the mudir only. The latter, obviously careful on the return to guide us into a bypath out of sight of the Senussi convent, walked quickly and nervously; but, once returned to his windowless room, became at ease, showing the keepsakes and trinkets with which he kept Stambuline life in mind in this wild place. He was a young Cypriote, mild-eyed, and, naturally, I should judge, of good parts and disposition; but full of wistful envy of Frankish culture, of which he had had a taste in boyhood at Nicosía, and in later youth at the French *lycée* of Galata. This kind of Turk makes rather a melancholy figure. Latin Europe does little for him beyond bringing *cafés chantants* and lewd photographs within his ken; and by robbing him of his implicit reliance on the law and custom of Islam, it throws him upon his own individuality, unsupported by the social code to which he was born. How, then, shall he keep his hands clean in some solitary seat of petty power? He may endure for a while; but, lacking pride of self and all faith, why should he refrain from picking and stealing and grinding the face of the poor? Hoping and approving the best way, he is bound sooner or later to follow the worst; and probably from his type develop the most evil of governors, those who are cruel for no other reason than that they feel weak and alone.

He was kind to us, however, putting all and sundry of his possessions at our service, even his single bedstead. But as the three of us would have filled a Great Bed of Ware, we settled precedence by stretching ourselves cheek by jowl on the floor; and so passed an unquiet night in the close air of the barred room. I slipped the bolts in the small hours of morning, and looked out over Cyrene. A pallid moon was sailing high within an iridescent ring, and mirk and scud were blowing up fast and faster from the west. We might count ourselves in luck if there were still some southing in the gale by the time we could reach the ship; but come what might, we must give a morning to Cyrene.

We began with the eastern cemetery, and were guided to the few painted tombs which earlier explorers have left unspoiled. The outer hall of the best shows a curious frieze of agonistic pictures in a very dim light. The funeral feasts and games, the foot races, chariot races, wrestling, and so forth, are rudely done in a late and coarse style; but they have this of interest, that many, indeed most, of the figures are painted of black complexion, while clad in gay Athenian garments.

There you have hybrid Cyrene, that colony which earliest made a practice of mixing Hellenic and barbarian blood, and had a history more Libyan than Greek. For the rest, we could do little more than visit a few larger tombs, and photograph the more curious of the pillared façades, which stand above the barley on the terraces; and though there was little light in the olive sky, we were able to get some pictures of the carved hillsides.

During three succeeding hours spent in rambling over the plateau above—hours which the poor mudir found slow-footed indeed—we learned how little of the great city is left above ground, and how much the excavators of 1861 left to be done. Murdoch Smith and Porcher, with the five blacks employed in their first season, and the thirty whom they considered a full gang in their second, did no more than scratch the skin of Cyrene. All that is most precious there, the spoil of the true Hellenic age, is still to seek. But the digger of the future, while enjoying greater security, will not have the free hand of the pioneers, for the Cretans are ploughing what the Senussi Arabs left fallow, and almost the whole site, when we saw it, stood thick with corn. So masked is it, at least in the spring-time, that the outline of the Stadium, the low ridge of the southern city wall, a few heaped up columns and other architectonic members of Byzantine churches, and the vast vaulted reservoirs of late Roman date are about all the ruins of whose character one can be sure in the eastern half of the city. Beyond the hollow, up which ran the main road from the Great Theatre and the Temple of Apollo, the western half of the site contains the Odeum or Smaller Theatre and a fine wreck of a

Hellenic tower, placed on the brink of the deep Wady Buhayat, at the point where the inward wall of the acropolis dips to join the outer wall of the city. The Roman castle stood at the north-western angle of Cyrene, which is the only point within the walls where the ground swells from the general level of the plateau into something like a hill. West, north, and east this angle breaks away in low cliffs, from whose foot the three main fountains of Cyrene spring, among them that of Apollo high up on the north-eastward face. With running streams on three sides, this commanding knoll seems alone to answer to that "place among waters" promised to the first colonists by the oracle; and if ever it be my fortune to search for the earliest Cyrene, I shall dig on that knoll, and not in the eastern city, where slopes are easy, and the spoil-heaps of former diggers alone break the level.

But here, as elsewhere, we scanned the few bare spaces in vain for potsherds of early style. Thick layers of late ruin and silt lie over them, and the three-foot corn-stalks stand above all. Only one noteworthy marble appeared on the surface, a pedestal with four reliefs, described by James Hamilton and other travellers. It is of fair workmanship, and inscribed with a greatly perished dedication not earlier than the age of the later Ptolemies. In the hollow between the two halves of the city, and over a wide area outside the walls, both south and north, innumerable dressed blocks stand upright, one behind another. With a field-glass one may see these puzzling files radiating from the city far out over the lower plain, ranged seemingly at random, as a baby might set toy bricks on end. I guessed at first they might be unwritten head-stones

THE APOLLO FOUNTAIN.

Facing p. 133.

of poor graves; but, seeing they occurred within the walls, and mostly in the lower lying places—for instance, about the upper part of the central hollow, below the vaulted reservoirs—I came to suspect they had once carried wooden pipes, which distributed the Apollo waters over the lower plain and the contents of the reservoirs to a part of the upper city; and I still can find no better reading of their riddle.

Our walk brought us at last to the Apollo fountain, the cause and centre of Cyrenian life. The cliff, from whose foot its stream flows forth, has been cut back and scarped. A gable-mark some twenty feet up its face bears witness that a portico once shadowed the basin, and a rock-inscription on the short returning face records its restoration in the early Imperial age. The stream can be followed upwards for some distance into the rock, if one cares to crawl among stalagmites; but the tunnel has narrowed since former days. The Bedawis say the water is each year less. As we drank of it and bathed our tired feet, we found it cool, not cold, and even on an April morning, in scirocco weather, only a few degrees below the air. Two or three Bedawis, who were washing their cotton garments, withdrew at our approach, and no women were visible. Other Bedawis, armed with long guns or spears and driving laden beasts, were passing to and fro on the path of the Senussi convent, the focus of modern Cyrene, which has created a broad belt of garden ground, frayed out over the lower plain.

Whatever may be dark regarding this Brotherhood, one thing at least is clear, that it has made the waste places of Cyrenaica bloom again, and fostered trade and settled life among the Bedawis. The Senussis "spare no effort," said James Hamilton in 1851, "to turn the property they have acquired (partly by purchase, but more largely by donation) to good account." Their convents are as much hostels as retreats, mansions where the Moslem wayfarer finds safety for his person and wares during at least three days. If the Arabs whom we met in Cyrene were dour and silent, so are almost all nomads at first sight of a stranger. They offered no sign of active hostility to us, who, for our part, were careful to keep outside the fence of the convent. We could see that the mudir hoped we would not transgress it; but in his frankest moments he spoke of Senussis not only without fear, but without any apparent sense that they mattered greatly. They were pious men, he said, the best of the local *Muslamin*, learned and peaceful. This particular convent of Ain Shahat got an evil name from the writings of Hamilton and Murdoch Smith, both of whom found the notorious long-living fanatic, Sidi Mustafa, in command; but when an Italian commercial mission reached Cyrene in 1884, it was received courteously by his successor.

On the whole, when one weighs what European travellers on the one hand, and educated Arabs on the other, have said about the Senussi Order, and also the known facts of its history since the founder, Sidi Muhammad, settled in Cyrenaica, one cannot but think that it has been taken too seriously in the West. The Order is not a sect, much less does it profess a religion of its own, for its members are of the Malekite school of Sunni believers. Only one confraternity among many in the world of Islam, it is sworn to practise a certain rigour of life—as an Arab understands rigour—in conformity with the letter of the Earliest Law; and, like most confraternities,

BEDAWIS OF THE BENI HAASA.

Facing p. 135.

it has assumed and paraded a certain secrecy. The founder had, however, this distinguishing idea, that the perfect life can best be led in temporal independence; and, therefore, he chose deserted Cyrenaica for the first home of his Order. As the Osmanli's grip tightened on the coast, and his braided officers became ubiquitous, Muhammad's successor, pursuing the same idea, withdrew from the district, first to the oasis of Jarabub in the southern waste, and then to Kufra. There he and his Order led a free and quiet life in the practice of pious exercises and the enjoyment of all pleasures which are not banned by the gospel of Gabriel—a life not too ascetic. Wine, tobacco, and coffee Senussis may not taste, but tea—what Word has forbidden it? That blessed drink, sings a poet of the sheikhly Senussi family, makes food sweet in the belly, and prolongs amorous passion; and what good things, he asks, need a man ensue more than these? It is credible that the Order, whether bidden from headquarters or inspired by local zeal, has kicked against the pricks now and then, and in doing what it could to stay the inroad of Christians, has set its face especially against Frenchmen in the Tunisian *hinterland*, and Britons in the Libyan oases and the western Sudan; but the painful withdrawals of the Senussi chiefs from the fair uplands of the coast farther and yet farther into torrid Africa have apparently been inspired only by a desire for a quiet Arabian life where Turks and Franks are not; and who shall blame them for that desire?

The local saints held themselves aloof, but a group of some forty armed Bedawis gathered to see us go. Squatting, eagle-beaked and narrow-eyed, like so many vultures on a rocky ledge, they set us thinking whether they could have found a use for their long guns and spears in some gully of the downward road, had we given them a little longer time for thought. As it was, we felt no fear, and gave back their stare. The Beni Haasa must be very pure Arab. I have noticed no finer type, even among the Bedawis who have come from Nejd itself within short historic memory. A few of their gipsy-like wives, seen not then but next day in the plain of Apollonia, showed the same high breeding in their unveiled faces.

The mudir added himself and his orderly to our cavalcade, and led us back briskly down the rock road towards the sea, the Syrian soldiers swinging alongside without any sign of tiring. Near the brink of the lower shelf we got glimpses right and left into the great gorges hewn in it, which have been for any number of ages haunts of cave-dwelling men; but their grandeur seemed to us somewhat below the enthusiasm of earlier travellers. Perhaps the thick, sunless air of that afternoon robbed them of their due effect. Perhaps we had come too lately from the splendid Lycian valleys and peaks to find the Cyrenaica all that those have found it whose eyes had first been blistered and blinded by the sun and sands of the Syrtis.

Our only fear was for the yacht. As we left the shelter of the forest and drew rein on the edge of the last steep, we knew how fierce a gale drove across the path. White wrinkles of surf alone betrayed the sea, for the mirk of the scirocco lay on the plain; and half an hour later, when we came to the Cretan huts, we could see no farther than the reefs, and had to be assured by the soldiers on the beach that the yacht was really gone. She had put out to sea the night before, they said, and appeared again with the sun; but since noon she had sheered off, and Allah knew where she might be now. If He willed, she had found peace behind Ras Hilal.

It was Wednesday at four of the afternoon, and not till Saturday, a little after midday, should we see her again. But for the doubt of her safety, which weighed most heavily on the Owner, and the certainty, to which we were all alive, that, should the gale haul to north or east of north, she must run from the Cyrenaic shore altogether, leaving us marooned for many days, we found ourselves in no very evil plight. True, we had slender baggage chosen for the needs of one night, not five; but how soon one forgets to change raiment even for sleep, and finds happiness far from a bath! The captain of the little post made over to us his guest-room, a roofed recess in a quarry, and thither his woman folk sent cushions and quilts, and trays of meat and rice and sticky pastry seasoned with curdled milk and garnished with herbs from the garden, which our host and the mudir helped us to clear with finger and thumb. There was good water; for the source a few miles inland, which used to keep Apollonia alive, has been led into an aqueduct again by the Cretans; and we found tobacco, which would at least burn, and *rahat*, peace, all the day long. What more, said the genial old soldier, do your hearts desire?

More, however, they did desire. We were Western men, with an itch to be doing, and we tried to fulfil our souls a little among the fallen churches and rock-tombs of Apollonia. But, with all our leisure, we made no great discovery there; and I doubt if the best thing we found were not wild watercress growing thickly in the conduit, which we taught the Cretans and the soldiers to relish. What is left of Apollonia is only a long landward slice of the city, which in Christian times outstripped dying Cyrene. All the seaward face of it, with the harbour-wall and gate and port, has been eaten by the waves. There is no doubt the coast has sunk here since Roman times, and is probably sinking still, and that the shallow bay, all rocks and shoals, in which we had made a difficult landing, is not any part of the old harbour of Apollonia, but was dry land when that harbour was sought by shipping. The reefs and islets, out at sea, over which the surf was now breaking so wildly, remain perhaps from the old foreshore. Further westward we found tombs into whose doors the waves flowed freely, and, had it been fairer weather, we might have espied others altogether submerged; for the calm sea on this coast is of such a wonderful clearness that when our leadsman was dipping for an anchorage on the first evening off Ras el-Tin, he could see a bottom of rock and sand, which, nevertheless, his plummet could not reach.

The ruins of two fine Apollonian churches are marked by magnificent monoliths of *cipollino*, which it would pay some marble merchant to ship away; but lack of moulded fragments and inscriptions shows that almost everything on the surface, except bits of black glazed pottery and stamped Samian ware, is of a very base age. Without powerful tackle one could not hope to get below that mass of fallen blocks, honeycombed by the blown sea salts. The landward wall, however, is in great part of the Greek time, remaining probably from the first foundation of the city, and seen from the hollow plain, it stands up finely. Somewhat, but not much later are

APOLLONIA IN STORM.

Facing p. 138.

the remains of an Ionic temple and of a theatre, which faces seawards without the wall. Here the work of the waves may be well admired, for the stage buildings are now awash and the surf runs up into the horseshoe of the seats.

The daily life of the little garrison was good to watch. The old commander had turned farmer. With the water-conduit under his control and thirty of the sturdiest knaves in the Levant at his orders, he was making more out of the red plain than any of the Cretans whom he had come to guard. The full privates hoed his garden: the corporal drove up his ewes at nightfall; and under the moon the old man himself would tuck his braided cuffs, tie half a dozen milky mothers head to tail, and tug at their teats. The soldiers, peasant conscripts born to such a life, seemed only too happy to go back to it, and the field-work filled their time and thoughts, and kept them in the rude health of shepherds.

Most of our time, however, we spent in watching sea and sky and uttering hopeful prophecies, which were slow to be fulfilled. All the scirocco died out of the weather by the first midnight, and a hard north-wester brought a livelier air, with rain and thunder and an ever-rising sea. By the third morning a surf was running both within and without the reefs, in which only a well-manned life-boat could have lived; and at last, unwillingly resigning hope that the yacht would return to take us off, we did what should have been done at least a day earlier—we found a trusty Bedawi, and sent him eastward down the coast to Ras Hilal. He came back at evening with a scrawl from our skipper, and the Owner ate a heartier meal than he had made yet in Marsa Susa.

With the fourth dawn the wind was falling, but the

sea ran very high still. The old Turk spoke of *rahat* for yet another day, but we would have no more of it; and, yielding to our entreaty, he called out an escort, and led us eastward to find the ship. There proved to be a fair path, used by the Cretans when they go to Derna. One of the refugees went ahead of us on a huge bull-camel, which could pick his way among rocks, and stride up the sides of gorges like a camel of Anatolia. When the track entered a wood, the rider would swing himself off by the first overhanging bough, and get back to the saddle again from the last, while his great beast never paused, feeling the burden of him hardly so much as to know if he were off or on. Much of the path led over red soil and under wild charubs and conifers, but thrice it was cut by sheer gullies, whose glassy limestone sides were bossed as if glaciers had passed. Two Bedawi tents were all the habitations we saw, and neither man nor woman was met; but once the path turned sharply to avoid a cluster of many graves, of which one was fresh mould. The tenting folk seem to bury in one spot, and not at hazard, as one might expect; and, indeed, they carry their dead many days' journey to particular wayside cemeteries. Would they spare the Awakening Angel the labour of collecting stragglers on the Last Day, or do the dead Bedawis love council and coffee-fellowship as much as the living?

On the cliffs of Ras Hilal we bade good-bye to the clean-living fellows who had escorted us and quietly refused our rewards. Gladly would the Owner have done them the honours of his ship, but this their old captain would not allow. In the latter's debt, too, we remained; for after he had been got aboard the swinging, pitching yacht at risk of a broken leg or a cracked skull, he pleaded to be let go again at once, and was put with difficulty back on shore. The western current which sweeps this iron-bound coast, was holding the ship broadside to the seas, and with wind and wave coming hour by hour more directly from the north, the open bay of Marsa Hilal was no place to ride in longer. Steam was got up, a course was set for Sicily, and by sunset the mountain of Cyrene lay on the horizon like a low cloud.

CHAPTER VII.

DIGGING.

THE search for ancient things below ground appeals to most minds, but especially to those of women, who are moved even more than men by curiosity and the passion of hazard. But few whose interest it excites seem to understand how rare are the high lights of success and how many the low lights of failure in a faithful picture of a digger's life. When I have been presented by a vague hostess as a "digger in the Levant," and we are between fish and flesh, my neighbour, glancing at my hands, will usually ask if my calling is a painful one in those climes. I reply that I dig *per alios*, and (with some shame) that, myself, I could not ply pick or spade anywhere for half a day. Incontinently she protests she could wish for nothing better than to lead such a life as mine. Whereupon, as best I may, I change the subject, not in fear she be as good as her word, but despair of giving her or any other inexpert person in that company and amid dinner table talk an understanding of the real nature of the digger's trade.

Indeed it is of such infinite variety, according to where, when, and why it happens to be followed, that generalities, even hedged about by all the caution of a leisured writer, are vanity: and the best I can do for you, my dinner partner, and for others who have felicitated me on the fascinating holidays which I spend in the Near East, is to describe briefly and, if I can, faithfully, the course of my two latest excavations. They were both typical of the digger's life, the first carried out among the foundations of a great Hellenic shrine, the second in a cemetery of Egypt; and both were fortunate and fruitful beyond common measure. The one began in the summer during whose early days I had been at Cyrene (brief respite I had that year!), the other fell eighteen months later, and to each I was commissioned by the British Museum.

Wood, the discoverer of the site of the great Artemisium at Ephesus, achieved the all but impossible in lighting on its pavement, which had been buried under twenty feet of silt, and performed a feat not less to his credit in opening out thereafter an area as large as the floor-space of a great cathedral. But when he left the site in 1874, he had manifestly not found all that remained of the most famous of ancient temples; nor of what he did indeed find would he ever compose a sufficient record. For thirty years doubts remained which the first Museum in the world, owner of the site, could not well refuse to resolve; and to resolve them I was sent to Ephesus in the last days of September, 1904.

The site looked then as hopeless as an ancient site can look—an immense water-logged pit choked with a tangled brake of thorns and reeds; and when axe and billhook and fire had cleared the jungle, it looked, if possible, more hopeless still. The shallow surface waters, however, when no longer sheltered by leafy canopies, dried quickly under the early October sun, and

I got to work with little delay on the platform of the temple which King Croesus had helped to build. A hundred men were enrolled, and every local means of carriage was pressed into their service. I got mule-carts and horse-carts, asses with panniers and asses with sacks, barrows and close-woven country baskets to be borne by boys. A central way was cut through the hillocks of marble, and from right and left of it broken stuff was sent up the ramps to dumping-grounds on the plain. But we were only reopening an earlier explorer's clearance, and could hope for little strange or new among his leavings. Not twice in a ten hour day did a scrap of carved or written stone, unseen or unsaved by Wood, reward our painful levering of tumbled blocks and sifting of stony soil. A common ganger with a hundred unskilled navvies could have served science as well as we.

As the polyglot labourers—half a dozen races chattered in the gangs—learned the ways of their taskmaster and became handy with their tools, the daily round grew ever more same, and each hour longer and emptier than the last. The beginning of an ambitious excavation is inspirited by an interest independent of results achieved or hoped. There are the local nature of the soil and the local peculiarities of the ancient remains to be learned: you have new and unhandy human instruments to temper, sharpen, and set: confidence must be gained and community of hope engendered. The days will go briskly for a week, two weeks, three weeks, according to the difficulties to be overcome. Then, if the instinct of the gamester be your mainstay in the digging trade, you will begin to crave winnings or, at least, the fair chance of them. Should there be some well-guarded kernel of the site, some presumed lode of antiquarian ore, you will endure still, performing hopefully the monotonous tasks of the digger's duty, while pick and shovel and knife are cutting onwards or downwards towards the hidden treasure; and if you can make your men comprehend and share your hope, the work will go forward well enough, with a fillip now and again from trifling loot found by the way. But if hope is deferred overlong, yet more if you have never held it confidently or never held it at all, your lot will insensibly become one of the dreariest that can fall to man. The germ of your hopelessness, infecting your labourers, will be developed more virulently in them. Their toil will lack life, and their tasks be scamped and vamped; their eyes will see not or their hands will not spare the evanescent relics of the past, while tired voices of their taskmasters rise and fall over their listless labour.

Many excavations I have seen—most indeed—go forward thus for a longer or a shorter time: and, since sometimes they cannot go forward otherwise, I have almost envied that sort of scientific excavator, generally Teuton, who seems to feel little or nothing of the gamester's goad, and plods on content to all appearance with his maps or his plans or his notes or nothing in particular, that might not be done better in his German study; while his labourers, clearing monuments that could not be missed in the dark by the worst trained observer in the world, shovel earth and stones like machines day in and day out for months together, and send them down a tramway under an overseer's eye. I say I have almost envied his content; but I always remember in time that, in digging, you only find if you care to find, and according to the measure of your caring; or, as a famous and fortunate explorer once put it, you find what you go out to find; and reckoning the momentary joy of success against the slow sorrow of failure, I rate the quality of the first so immeasurably more worth than the quantity of the last, that I am consoled. If lack of luck vexes the gamester's soul, it is to him that the rare prizes of hazard most often fall.

October passed away thus, and November was on the wane; but no prize had appeared to lighten our weary days. Already we had pierced the platform at several points to meet with nothing better below it than sand and water. What, in reason, was to be hoped above it, where diggers from Justinian's day to Wood's had rummaged and robbed? We cajoled despair with the most insignificant discoveries—with patches of bare pavement, with scraps of Roman inscriptions chipped out of masses of Byzantine concrete, with a few sherds of Greek vases and broken terra-cottas sifted out of the bedding of the temple-steps built in Alexander's day. In a world where the absolute is never attained, the relative, thank heaven! can always please, and Nature, of her pity, with a little of your contributory good will, will blind you to relativity.

No other antiquarian work could be done elsewhere to fill the days. The rest of the site of Ephesus, city, suburbs, and district, had been conceded to an Austrian Mission which was even then present in full force, exploring the great market-place and its southern approach, as well as the famous double Church of Mary Mother of God. Its distinguished leaders, greatly though they had desired the Artemisium site for their own, treated me from the first with all sympathy and courtesy, and the least return I could make was to respect all their wide preserves. Now and then I visited their work, which was proceeding almost as uneventfully as my own, and rode an aimless round on the Cayster plain and the dusty hills. Rarely I received visitors who were politely contemptuous of my sodden pit, and every day I watched the slow fall of the leaf in the fig orchards of Ayassolúk.

The last days of November came. The platform of Wood's "earliest temple" was almost cleared, and several shafts had been sunk fruitlessly through its massive foundations. To go on with such work in a second season would be to waste time and money, and it seemed best to make an end in one campaign by keeping the men through December into January. The gang, which was clearing the central sanctuary, had reached its midway point and begun to lay open the meagre remains of a small oblong structure, which Wood had named the "Great Altar," and left undisturbed. I noted that it had only an outer skin of marble, and was filled in solid with small limestone slabs. So far we had sunk no pits through the pavement of the sanctuary itself, though many in the peristyle; and where better might we probe than in the heart of this "Altar," where no massive foundations would have to be broken through? Moreover, we might hope to learn whether the structure were indeed a "Great Altar" or not rather the pedestal of the divine image which was set up in the Holy of Holies.

The topmost slabs were lifted easily out of their beds: and not less easily those of a second layer. Gazing dully at their prints on the mud-mortar I noticed some bright specks, and stooping, picked out two or three. They were flakes of leaf-gold, fallen from some gilded object which had perished, whatever it was. But no sooner was the first slab of a third layer raised than something better than a flake of foil shone on its bed, namely a little plate of impure gold, stamped with a geometric Ionian pattern, and pierced at the corners. I thought of the goddess who had stood in effigy on this pedestal, of her plated diadem and gold-encrusted robe, and sent for sieves.

For the rest of that day hours passed as minutes. Every handful of mud mortar washed through the meshes left treasure behind—women's gauds for the most part, earrings of all patterns and weights, beads of sundered necklace-strings, pins for the hair, and brooches for the shoulder or throat, some of these last fashioned after the likeness of hawks in the finest granular work of Ionian smiths. With them appeared primitive electrum coins, fresh from the mint. I was as puzzled as pleased. How had delicate jewels come to lurk there, fresh and unspoiled? When the first specimens appeared, I thought them accidents of ruin—precious trappings of the statue carried down by water through chinks of its pedestal, or, perhaps, contents of some perished casket. But such possibilities became impossible as the jewels continued to be found in each successive bed of mortar. It grew clear that we had chanced on some sort of foundation deposit—on objects hidden with a purpose when the first builders were laying course on course of the pedestal, and that we had the most desired of treasures, fine work of the Ionian spring-time of Greece. Perhaps also we had solved at last the mystery of Greek foundation-deposits. Under Egyptian temples Petrie has found many such deposits, whether beneath corner stones, or the main threshold, or in the central axis of a building; but under Greek shrines the hiding place of foundation records had never yet been divined. Yet what spot more fitting than the pedestal of the most sacred statue at the very heart of the sacred plan?

We had dug out only a small part of our vein of treasure when dark came down with a rising gale, whose fierce squalls brought up the long expected rains. On and off, at some hour of every day and night, it would rain for a week and more, sometimes with lightning and cyclonic winds, sometimes in sodden calm. The storms which had begun in unnatural warmth continued, after the third day, in cruel cold, which coated the pools with ice, and froze the very marrow of the men who had to grope for jewels waist-deep in water and slime; but we dared not pause for even a day. The fame of our find had gone abroad, and others would have dredged had we not. The blue fingers of the men cracked and swelled with washing sharp shingle in the sieves till they could hardly pick out jewels, and I knew what it was to be wet through and chilled through for a week on end.

During a momentary brightening of the sky we sank pits outside the pedestal, and there too found foundations of walls earlier than our predecessors had found, and fragments of fine Ionian things lying among them. Then down again came the deluge to flood the pits. For eight days we fought the weather, replacing the worn-out and sick with eager volunteers. Each morning the water had risen above its morning level of the day before, and at last it began to well up faster than we could bale. The rains of winter had come in earnest, and we must await spring. The hole which we had made in the pedestal was choked again with blocks too heavy for furtive marauders to drag out, so long as water lay deep around, and before the middle of December I had gone to Constantinople carrying more than half a thousand jewels. Whatsoever of the goddess's treasure might be buried still was left to the keeping of watchmen and the flood.

The waters guarded their trust. That winter is yet remembered in Anatolia for its rains and the fevers which followed. When I returned to the site near the end of March, I looked out over a lake below whose unruffled surface the pedestal lay drowned too deep for anyone but a diver to rob its core, and its upper stones, said the Ephesians, would not emerge till late summer. What was to be done? The water could not be drained out of that great hollow, which lies many feet below the general level of the plain and hardly higher than the surface of the distant sea, except by the help of a very powerful steam pump. I left a contractor to clear away the upper part of Wood's great rubbish heaps, which still blocked the two ends of the site, and went back to Smyrna.

To make a long story short, an engine and pump were lent by the Ottoman Railway Company and dragged to the edge of our pit three weeks later; and after we had cut a passage seaward for the strong stream which its twelve-inch pipe would disgorge, it was set to work to lower the lake. But we were only at the beginning of difficulties. The upper waters were sucked up in a few hours; but the drainage of the lower levels, which were dammed by deep and massive foundation walls, could not be collected fast enough to keep

RIGGING THE GREAT PUMP AT EPHESUS.

Facing p. 150.

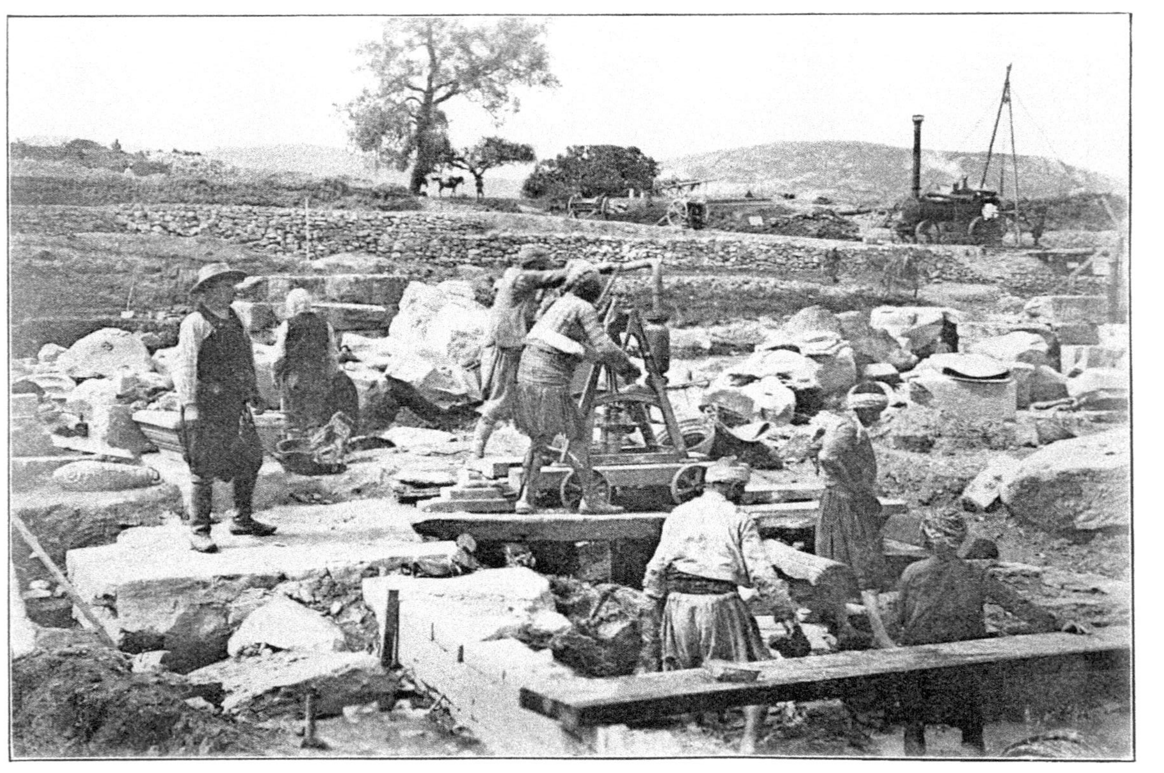

THE TREASURE SPOT AND PUMPS.

Facing p. 151.

the great pipe free of air, and unchoked by mud. If the engine stopped, the waters ceased to flow towards it, and in the lapse of a night the pond would rise nearly as high again as at the first. There was nothing for it but to spend many days in cutting a network of channels through the foundations and in deepening the pool below the pipe by hauling out great rubble blocks which had been bedded down by the builders of the latest temple. The men, who had to wade to their middles under a hot sun, fell sick of fevers, and I myself began to feel none too well. On the last day of April I took to my bed, and after fighting my malady for a week, went down to Smyrna in high fever and was put to bed in the Seamen's Hospital for other ten days. Thus it was not till May was half gone that, with drainage channels dug, the central area of the temple fenced against inflow, and a second and smaller pump rigged over the treasure-spot, we could hunt again for jewels.

They appeared one after another in the sieves just as they had done five months before; and when the clean bottom sand had been scraped out of the four corners of the pedestal, we had added nearly five hundred trinkets. But now I cared for none of these things. The fever had left me unstrung, and I longed for nothing but the moment when I might scrape Diana's mud off my feet for the last time. Every evening I hoped against hope that the lode would be exhausted next day. I have never struck such a vein of luck, and never liked my luck less. The site, it must be allowed, was no place for a hardly convalescent man. The end of May approached. Each noon the sun beat more fiercely into our windless hollow, and the flood, which was sucked out by the great pump each morning, left tracts of slowly drying slime and stranded water-beasts withering and stinking among rotten weeds. One could not watch the workmen without wading and mud-larking and groping in that fetid ooze. Every page of my diary breathes utter disgust of it and yearning for a cleaner, sweeter life. For all I cared, Science and Duty might go to the wall; and thither I had sent them and myself as well but for shame of old Gregóri and his cold, unsleeping eye. He had dug a dozen sites with me, and never yet stopped short of the bottom or refused to follow a likely lead. Was I going to tempt him now?

I did not. I held out, even to the dog days. Before the pedestal was exhausted we had begun to probe the mud about it, and there find ruins of three small shrines, one below the other, and many precious broken things in the slimy bottom of the lowest and earliest. These were rarely jewels and articles of personal wear like those that made up the Pedestal Treasure, but chiefly things used in worship, and fragments of votive offerings. These had not been hidden of set purpose where we found them, but were lost and forgotten things, sucked into the bottom ooze, or trodden under foot in some wild hour of ruin or sack. Since the earliest shrine on the site must be supposed founded not later than 700 B.C., it may well be we dredged from its nether slime treasures unseen since the sanctuary was violated by a rude Cimmerian horde in the reign of Ardys II. of Lydia. That these objects belonged to much the same period as the Pedestal Treasure, the artistic character of many bore witness: that, like that Treasure, they were of earlier date than the second of the three primitive shrines was proved by our finding certain of them bedded under its surviving foundations. In one case only did we seem to light on anything buried with intention. This was a little jar, set upright in an angle of the lowest foundations and once sealed with a covering, whose binding-cord still clung to the clay. My men were no longer in their first innocence, and dealers in contraband waited at noon and night to tempt them. He who first sighted this jar, as he was scraping slime into his basket, looked stealthily about him; but I was at his back, poor fellow, ready to lift his prize myself, and I see his sad eyes still as nineteen electrum coins of the earliest mintage of Lydia fell out of his pot.

We got statuettes, whole or broken, by the score, whether in ivory—priceless treasures these of early Ionian art—or in bronze, or in terra-cotta, or even in wood. We got vessels in ivory and vessels in clay. We got much gold and electrum, which had been used for casing or adorning things decayed: we got some silver, and, best prize of all, a plate engraved on both faces, in the oldest Ionic character, with a record of contributions towards a rebuilding of the shrine. We got many another object, broken or imperfect, but not less precious, in crystal and paste and amber and bronze. In sum, when all the ground had been searched, we had recovered from the treasures of the first House of Artemis in the Ephesian plain hard on three thousand objects, one with another and greater with less. I took them all to Constantinople, as in honour bound, for we had subscribed to the Ottoman Law and made no bargain with the Turk. But in return for our good faith, all the objects were suffered to go for a season to England to be ordered and studied.

I wanted nothing less than to see them again when I left Stambul, and nothing more than to keep them for ever in London, when, a year later, they had to return.

. . . .

The other excavation to be described was of that body-snatching sort, which Science approves and will doubtless justify to the Angel of the Resurrection by pleading a statute of limitations. To rob a tomb appears, in fact, to be held dastardly or laudable according as the tenancy of the corpse has been long or short. I once explored a Graeco-Roman cemetery near Alexandria with as willing a Moslem gang as heart could desire. But one of my men ate apart from his companions and had no fellowship with them. He was by far the best digger of them all; none so light of hand as he, so deft to extricate fragile objects from one grave, and to find his way into another. I foresaw a useful *reis*, and said so to the overseer. He listened in silence, and at evening asked leave to speak. The rest, he said, would leave me sooner than take orders from this man. He was a good tomb-digger; but where had he learned his trade? In the modern cemeteries of the town. He stole grave-clothes. I did not make him a *reis*, but paid him off next day—why or with what right I hardly know.

I was bidden to search the tombs in part of the hill behind Siut, whose soft calcareous cliffs are honey-combed with graves of every age. The vast cemetery, lying near a large town, has been ransacked over and over again, chiefly for wooden statuettes and models, which seem to have been carved more often and more cleverly at the Wolf Town than anywhere else in old Egypt; and I was warned I must hope for no untouched burials, but content myself with raking

A SEALED GRAVE-DOOR.

over the leavings of hastier robbers. The event belied the warning. First and last we had the fortune to find nearly thirty sealed graves, many poor enough, and some re-used for second and humble burials, but a few of the Old Empire period, whose furniture adorns even the rich collections in Bloomsbury. But it was with all the pain in the world, amid recurring failures, and after weeks of fruitless toil, that we found those. For every profitable tomb at least twenty profitless had to be opened and, moreover, examined scrupulously, since it was hardly ever possible to be sure if the dead man had been wholly robbed till we reached his chamber itself, ten to thirty feet below the surface. The deep shaft of entry would often seem as the masons had left it in the distant days of the Twelfth Dynasty, filled to its brim with their clean limestone chips; but none the less the coffins would be found at the last smashed or removed, the best of the furniture withdrawn, and the rest heaped pell-mell in utter ruin, after the chamber had been entered from below by a passage rudely hewn from a neighbour grot. Yet even then it could not be abandoned unsearched; and for other and many days the men must turn over the piles of earth and bones and scraps in faint hope that something of value had been overlooked or despised by earlier robbers. Doing this slow, blind work, they must needs be watched by the dim light of smoky candles in the choking dust-laden air of a narrow cell, which reeked of mummy clothes and the foul rags of *fellahin*. Had I been an annual digger in Egypt, able to call a trained and trusted crew to Siut, and had the scene not lain so near a large town notorious for its illicit traffic in antiques, that penance might have been avoided. And even in performing it one was robbed. Dealers waited for my men at sunset below the hill and beset them all the way to the town, and one digger, a youth of brighter wit and face than most—he was half a Bedawi—gained so much in the few weeks before I turned him off that he bought him a camel, a donkey and a wife. The order of his purchases was always stated thus, whoever told the tale.

The most bitter disappointment was caused by a great collapsed grotto through whose choked portal we had quarried our way to find the central grave-pit still covered with its lid of ancient palm-trunks. We lifted these and dug into the clean chips below with ever brighter hopes; for the shaft was so virgin that the white dust made by the original chiselling hung still on its walls. Down and down the men delved, keen as their masters, and for five-and-twenty feet into the depths of the hill the filling was pure of all sign of disturbance. Then at last the chamber appeared, doorless, pure and empty as the shaft. The tomb had never been used for burial at all.

So success seemed to flee before us, and to pursue it was dangerous, where rock was rotten and screes of loose chips, thrown out from plundered tombs above, might slip at any moment over the only channels of air and escape, and condemn us to the death of trapped rats in a most unworthy cause and most unpleasant company. Crawling on all fours in the dark, one often found the passage barred by a heap of dim swaddled mummies turned out of their coffins by some earlier snatcher of bodies; and over these one had to go, feeling their breast-bones crack under one's knees and their swathed heads shift horribly this way or that under one's hands.

And having found nothing to loot in a thrice plundered charnel-house, one crawled back by the same grisly path to the sunlight, choked with mummy dust and redolent of more rotten grave-clothes than the balms of Arabia could sweeten. Partner of the scented dinner-table, is that the trade you desire?

And how would our evening hours have seemed to you? They were spent in a huge grotto with storied walls, because the lower Nile valley is a thoroughfare of furious winds all the winter long, and tent life, a constant misery in Egypt, would have been most miserable on the face of the Siut bluff, which stands out into the winds' track, and is buffeted by all their storms. Not that our wide-mouthed grotto, however, proved much better than a tent. The north wind struck its farther wall, and was sucked round the other two in an unceasing, unsparing draught which dropped dust by the way on everything we ate or drank or kept. Warmth after the day's toil we never felt from December to February, even when sitting closest to the fire which we kindled nightly with unpainted slats of ancient coffins on a hearth of Old Empire bricks. The dead wood, seasoned by four thousand years of drought, threw off an ancient and corpse-like smell, which left its faint savour on the toast which we scorched at the embers; and a clear smokeless light fell fitfully on serried coffins, each hiding a gaunt tenant swathed and bound, to whose quiet presence we grew so little sensitive that we ranged our stores and bottles, our pans and our spare garments on his convenient lid.

None the less—I will avow it, dear lady, even if I wake after all your desire to dig—I used to put all these ills, the disappointments and discomforts of the work and life, to the account of things that matter not at all every time that I watched the clearance of a sealed tomb-door. I have dug for twenty years and set next foot after the sexton's in very many ancient sepulchres; but I still feel, as at first, the flutter of poignant hope that the tomb may be virgin, and an indescribable thrill at the sight of grave furniture undisturbed since thousands of years. There lie the dead man's bow and arrows in their place on his coffin-lid, string snapped and plumes in dust, and there his stout staff and his boomerang: the little Nile boats are propped fully manned by his side; the wooden servants who answer his call in the underworld are at their several businesses: and his effigy, with his wife's, stands at his head. I know well that, in Egypt at least, one hardly ever opens a perfectly virgin sepulchre. Someone robbed it on the night of the burial ere the door was sealed. Some malign intruder has rumpled those grave clothes down to the waist in quest of the jewels on neck and breast, and has trampled or overturned in his guilty haste the furniture beside the coffin. But since he withdrew with his accomplices and sealed the door, all has been silence and fine rain of dust from the roof, until, after four thousand years, *you* come. You may talk of science and think of loot, while the chattering diggers are working like fiends to lift the last of the filling from the shaft; but the first look into the dimness of the sepulchre itself will silence them, hardened robbers though they be, and will silence you. Science and your own glory and the lust of loot are all forgotten in the awe which falls as in fairy tales on adventurers in underground chambers where kings of old time sit asleep. Yet next day, or maybe the day after, when that coffin has been packed with twenty others in the magazine,

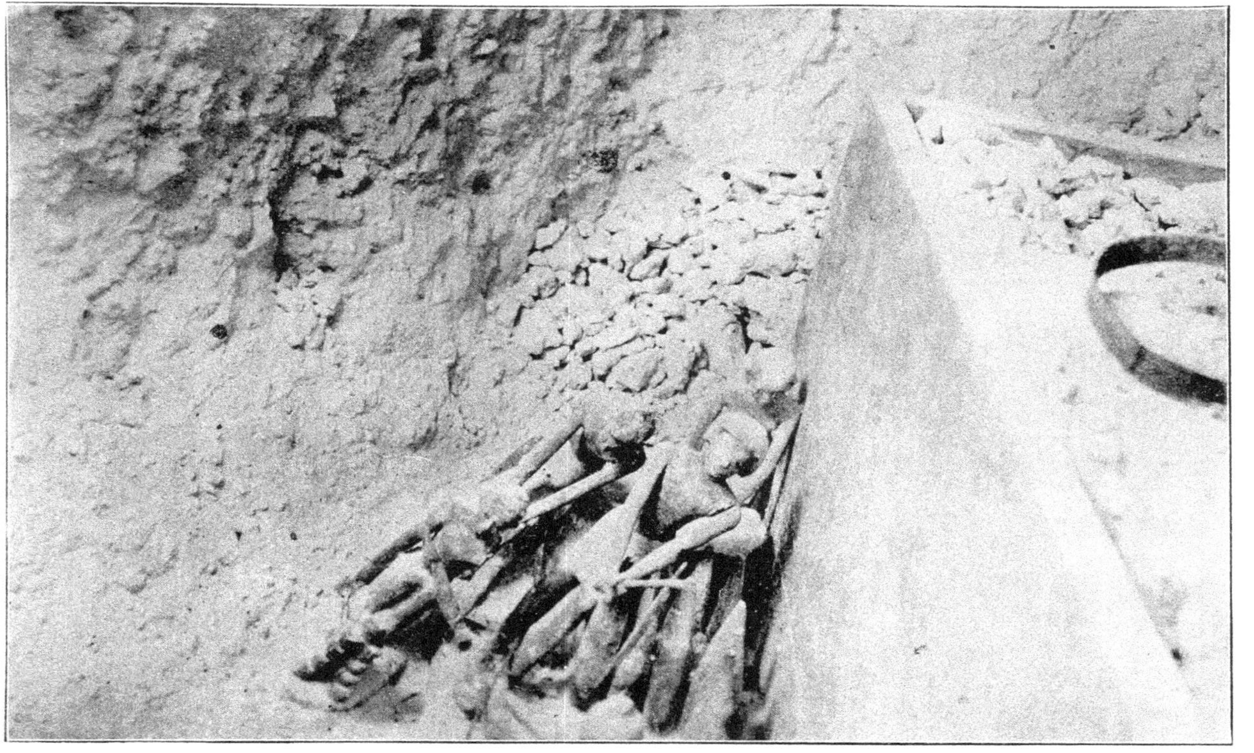

MODELS OF SERVANTS AT THEIR WORK BESIDE A COFFIN.

Facing p. 158.

you will play cards of an evening on its head, if it happens to be handy.

Not too nice a trade, you see, dear lady. Best let it be!

CHAPTER VIII.

THE SAJUR.

It rained in the Syrian March of 1908 when it did not snow, and wet or fair it blew a gale. We came to Aleppo in a deluge, wallowed in mud at Mumbij, found Euphrates swinging in full flood round his mighty curves, crossed him before a wet gale, recrossed and rode all the way to Aintab head down to the same laden blast. Sleet and snow, rain and hail spent themselves in turn on that highland town during four miserable days. But on the fifth morning the sky was clear. The tracks had hardened in one fair night, and bush and tree were eager for spring. When we wheeled on the crest of a low pass for a last look into the sunlit valley, a far-away frame of dazzling peaks had risen where clouds were hanging yesterday. Life was sweet once more, and the world seemed good.

The hope of hunters beckoned us ahead. A fortnight ago, while we lay in camp by Carchemish, a friendly Syrian had promised two things, first, "black written stones" near a village two hours to the north; second, "writing like nails," to be seen on the farther bank of Euphrates over against the outfall of the Sajúr. The first promise had been fulfilled, and the black stones of Kellekli were put to our credit. The second promise

EUPHRATES FROM THE MOUND OF CARCHEMISH.

Facing p. 160.

we were now on our way to prove. A mound called Tell Ahmar was marked on our maps opposite the mouth of the Sajur, and there we would look for the Syrian's "nail-like" writing, which could hardly mean other than the wedge-shaped script of the Assyrians. Cuneiform records would be worth the finding on the frontier of the Hatti land.

Moreover, there might be quarry on the road. On this first night we should camp under Tell Bashár, known to historians of the Crusades as a great mound by the Sajur, whither the Frank lords of Edessa betook themselves when driven back across Euphrates. When I passed through Aintab for the first time, fifteen years ago, I found in its bazars and khans sundry Hittite seals and trinkets, which were said by their vendors to have been found, one and all, on Tell Bashar. I doubted their story then, knowing how natives will combine to say that small antiquities come from the most notable ruin in their district, whatever its age; but with wider knowledge of Syria I began to believe. Few or no mounds so large as this was reported to be, have ever been built up from the level by Franks. Rather as at Aleppo and Hamah and a score of other places the Crusaders, like the Moslems before and after them, set their towers on old mounds of the Hittites. It was worth while, at least, to spend a night in some hamlet near the Tell, and enquire diligently if such trinkets had indeed been found there by husbandmen and shepherds, or were hanging yet on the neck-strings of their wives.

I had met with no record of any antiquary's visit to Tell Bashar, and the place was reported to us in Birejik and Aintab to be a spot where a stranger would not be well received. The nearest village was a home of outlaws with whom the Pasha meant to deal faithfully, *bukra*, to-morrow, or may be next day, or may be next year. But the outlaw in Turkey is more often a friend than a foe to wandering sahibs who may make his peace for him some day, and we rode on. Many laden camels were in the road—we were still on the bridle path which leads to Aleppo—and their drivers greeted us in friendly fashion, as glad as we of the unaccustomed sunlight and new-washed air : but each man carried his ready gun. Presently our way parted from the main track, and bore south by east over a deep hill-girt plain to the banks of a little canal, unwonted sight in Turkey of Asia. Here at least men live who take thought for the morrow, and in a land of ancient violence, hold something better than to rob and kill. We sighted a few women, bent over the wet earth in their daily quest for liquorice root, but no near villages; and when we halted at noon by a double spring, no one came near us except two curious herd-boys. The traveller in Turkey, who must eat most of his bread at noon and night amid the odours of villages and under the unflinching regard of scornful eyes, remembers with blessing his rare meals by wayside fountains. There he has no questions to answer and none to ask. The sunshine is his, and his the best of the shade. Lolling at his western ease, with no eastern punctilio to bear in mind, he forgets for a moment those twin spoilsports of the Levant, suspicion and bakshish.

We had remounted and ridden forward for less than an hour, when the low eastern range ran out into a second plain and a great mound sprang out of the flats ahead. Needless to ask if it were Tell Bashar. Longer, broader, and higher than the acropolis of Carchemish, it had the same abrupt flat-topped form, and even at our distance could be seen to rise between the horns of a low crescent of mounds, which kept the line of some city's buried wall. We rode over the Sajur by the high-pitched bridge of Sarambol which has carried the mule-track from Aleppo to Birejik for centuries; and, having cut across an elbow of the meandering stream, we recrossed to the village of Bashar, and chose a camping ground on sodden grass beyond its huts. The sheikh called us to his upper chamber, and we took coffee amid a gathering throng of peasants who seemed willing enough to further our desires, but could muster only a defaced coin or two after a two-hour sitting, and tell us nothing of Hittite seals. Our hopes sank low. But the evening and the morning, when shepherds and women are home from the fields, often bring forth that which the afternoon knows not; and we thought it well to leave the village to talk us over, while we went on to the site.

Huge the Tell loomed near at hand, as we rode through a green gap in the outer crescent of mounds, and the climb to its flat summit proved very steep. All that was to be seen thereon was work of the Franks—foundation lines of their halls and ramparts, choked cisterns of their making, and two fragments of towers that had kept their main entrance on the south side—with nothing of an earlier day unless it were certain black blocks of basalt, worked here and there into their masonry. From this height the outer mounds could be seen to enclose west, south and east a site larger than Carchemish, but alas! ploughed from end to end, and cleared of all stones, modern or ancient. On the north the ground falls steeply from the foot of the mound and stretches flat a hundred yards to the Sajur, whose sinuous reaches gleamed in the sinking sunlight. The river passes Tell Bashar in loops and counter-loops, fetching a wide compass to the east before finding its southward way again, and probably it has shifted its course continually in the soft, stoneless plain. The little fall of the land at the northern foot of Tell Bashar may well, therefore, be a forgotten bank, and the mound have risen, like other early fortresses, from the water's very edge.

It was an hour after sunset when the first-fruits of the harvest we sought appeared at our tent-door. They were two seals of steatite, gable-shaped and engraved, which had been strung on a woman's necklace in the company of modern charms to avert the 'eye.' No price was asked, but what we chose to give. We paid well, and had not time to finish supper before spoil of the Hittites—their cylinders, their beads, their seals, gable-shaped, conical, scarabaeoid—flowed in from all sides, and the source of the Aintab objects was beyond all doubt. So thick became the throng of vendors at last that the sheikh, attended by armed satellites, came up to close the market. He was nervous, and begged we would not sleep. His village, he protested, was bad, and some months before had fought a pitched battle for its lands, and killed some Aintablis. The Pasha's police had come to arrest the slayers, but been driven off, and the ringleaders, yet at large, had nothing to lose by an attack on our camp. He, the sheikh, would suffer if a hair of our heads was touched. We promised to be wary, and he went off, leaving his guards by the tents.

The night was bitterly cold. The north wind, which

THE SAJUR VALLEY AT SUNSET FROM TELL BASHAR.

Facing p. 164.

had so cheered our morning hours, did not die at sunset as is its wont, but blew on through the dark in token that the weather was not yet firm, and the sodden grass grew crisp under its breath. It was too chill for stripping, and almost too chill for sleep, and had robbers come at any hour of that night they would have found one or the other of us awake. But they came not, and I doubt if any had ever a mind to come. The peasants shewed us, first and last, as good hospitality as their poverty allowed, offering again and again their little cups of bitter coffee half filled in the Arab fashion, and at sunrise they came to the tents once more asking no higher prices than overnight. Collecting was too easy a business here to be a sport at all; but the bag consoled us. When we rode off to the south we had gathered in nearly sixty Hittite things. Few women in that little village had not hung a cylinder or a seal on their necklaces to win ease in childbed, and make the milk sweet in their breasts, and I trust they have found others of equal virtue to replace those for which two Franks were so ready to pay their silver.

Records of Shalmaneser II. mention a notable fenced place, situated on the river *Sagura* and taken once and again by the Great King on his forays across Euphrates. He names it, in his long-winded Ninevite way, Ashur-utir-asbat; but, he says, "the Hatti call it Pitru." By the latter name the Pharaohs of the Eighteenth Dynasty also knew a strong city of northern Syria, which lay on their way to Carchemish. The site of Pitru on the Sagura has never been fixed; but no one before us with Pitru in his mind had seen Tell Bashar, which is by far the largest ancient site on the Sajur. If Til-Barsip, where

Shalmaneser crossed Euphrates, was indeed at modern Birejik, as Assyriologists believe, be it noted that Tell Bashar lies on the straightest road from this point to Halman, or Aleppo, whither the King marched from Pitru in the year before Christ, 854. That diggers will prove some day that Pitru and Bashar are one, I make small doubt; but I feel less sure that, as some of those who study the geography of the old Hebrew world think, Pitru was also the same town as that Pethor "in Aram in the mountains of the east"; whence Balak the Moabite called Balaam to curse Israel. Pethor is said elsewhere to have been of Aram Naharaim, or Mesopotamia; but the Hebrew scribes were not scientific geographers, and I will leave another dark saying of theirs concerning Pethor, that it was "by the river of the land of the children of Balak's people," to the Higher Critics. Nevertheless, if ever there be a plan afoot to dig Tell Bashár, one might invoke reasonably enough the name of the son of Beor to open purses which are usually closed to diggers unashamed to beg.

Our second day by the Sajur passed cloudless as the first, and the land still kept the festival of yesterday. The ride over the treeless rolling downs would be dreary enough in mirky weather; but on that day the shallow dales rejoiced in the sun, the brooks laughed as we forded them, the sheep flecked emerald slopes, and wherever there was tilth, the young wheat showed an even brighter green. So crystal clear was the air that the freshly powdered peaks of Amánus stood up boldly in the west as though ten, instead of sixty miles away, and from every higher swell of the downs we got a backward view to yet more distant snows on Taurus. The very pack-horses, sorry jades that they were, felt the spur of spring:

they hinnied, squealed, headed off the track to gallantry and combat, till at last they broke into a frenzy of kicking and galloping which brought their packs about their heels and their panting drivers' fists about their heads. A packhorse, who fancies himself Pegasus, is the most laughable beast on earth till he begins to scatter your bedding, your instruments, your garments and your food over a mile of rock or bog.

Low bluffs of basalt ran for a long distance on our left, in which quarries of the Hittites will be found some day; for tooled blocks of their black stone were scattered over both a small mound passed on the way, and a much larger acropolis which we spied at noon in the trough of a tributary valley. Tell Khalid is the second site on the Sajur for size, and must survive from some town known to Assyrian history. In a hamlet on the farther bank of the stream, which was reached by plunging through almost too swollen a flood, we were bidden rest and eat by the Bey, a friendly Mussulman, rich in beautiful brood mares, which were browsing unshackled with their young on lawn-like pastures; and during this short stay, the peasants had time to bethink them of three or four trifles picked up at one time or another on their mound—of a scarabaeus in paste, two engraved seals, some haematite beads, and, more welcome than these, a terra-cotta figurine of the Goddess of Syria, pressing her breasts in the manner of Ishtar.

Well pleased we rode on in the early afternoon to the bridge of the Sajur at Akjé, where rumour had it we might lodge in a khan. But the khan proved ruinous, like the bridge, and empty of all but dung and fleas, since the waggons bound from Aleppo to Mesopotamia have ceased to pass this way; and we had no choice but to keep on, parted by the stream from a chain of villages on the left bank, each built on or by an ancient mound. After an hour and a half we reached a spot marked on the maps a hamlet, Kubbeh, but in reality a large farmstead with attendant hovels and a water-mill, owned by a wealthy Aleppine who lives away till the summer-time. His bailiff, a grave, black-bearded man, bade us welcome with respectful eyes, and abased himself even to draw off our shoes. We lay comfortably in the Bey's chamber, and on the morrow went our way his debtors. The old feudal families may be extinct or reduced to shadows in Turkey; but the spirit of feudal dependence is as strong as ever in the country folk. Instinctively the peasants gather about a rich man's dwelling, be he only a tax-farmer—as indeed were most of the "Deré Beys"; and they would rather be his vassals than small proprietors on their own lands. Traditions of ancient lawlessness and present fear of strong men, armed by the law, do something to keep this habit alive: but its roots lie deeper—deep down in that immemorial respect of persons which goes in the East with a fixed belief that they are respected by the Most High.

The third morning broke grey, with a chill wind off the Mesopotamian desert and a threat of rain; but the weather held fair till we halted in the village of Dadat at noon. We had kept to the more mountainous right bank, though, for more than one long stretch, we found no beaten way. Most villages were seen, to-day as yesterday, on the farther side, and it would have been easier to have crossed the stream and journeyed on their linking paths. But the map showed an earlier traveller's track on the left bank, while it left the right blank, both of roads and villages (although we lighted on two as considerable as the largest of those opposite), and it seemed better to strike out a new route. The river kept us company, tumbling down a long and gently inclined ladder of rock, with short reaches of stiller water, in which herons waded, careless of our passing by: but beyond Dadat we saw it bear away to north, hugging the hills, and were warned that sheer bluffs would bar any farther riding by its bank.

It had begun to rain when we struck off over the downs, in hopes to reach shelter at the village of Chat ere the storm should become heavy. Two Turkman camps lay on our way, and the elders of the tents, as soon as persuaded we were no robbers, gave us guidance through a maze of tortuous sheep-tracks. Cold looked the black booths flapping in the searching easter, colder the rolling treeless down on which the wanderers' lives were led, coldest the scudding wrack in the sky. All joy of yesterday had forsaken the world, and we hailed the hovels of Chat as a sailor hails a port. But Chat did not hail us. We were many men and more horses, and the best shelter was already over-full of wives and children and cattle, among whom a narrow space was not very willingly cleared for us. While he burned an armful of thorns in the chimney, the Headman pointed to the thinning clouds, and protested another village lay just beyond the hill.

Ready to be persuaded, we went farther to fare worse. Once on the downs again we met the full fury of the soaking, freezing gale. There was no pretence of a path, and the dusty hillsides were already become bog and slime. A horse slid, plunged, and broke his girths, then another and another; and the dusk came down so fast that only the very last of the light served us into Avshariyeh, as mean a knot of cabins as one may see even in Syria. The one guest-house was packed with travellers, Circassian, Arab and Turk, who had been ferried over Euphrates in the afternoon; and no man had so much as an empty stable to offer. It was idle, however, to plead there would be better lodging in some farther village, for, less than a mile ahead, the Great River barred our way in the night; and there was but one course open —boldly to enter the sheikh's dwelling and occupy till he came in the sacred name of hospitality, and the more potent name of the Frank. It was a large stone-built barn, three parts stable, with a small living space raised and railed, which we took for ourselves without more ado. The women and children scurried into the dark of the stable end: their old lord followed us, and accepting the inevitable, began forthwith, Arabwise, to revolve in his slow mind how the chance might be turned to profit. He too, it appeared, was a stranger in the land, going in fear of the Circassian farmers on the royal estate of Mumbij, and he had a likely son. Here were *Ingliz* by his hearth, *Ingliz* who, their escort said, stood very near to the great Consul in Aleppo. If they spoke for his boy, would he not be made *kavass*, and, by the custom of generations, a rock of defence for all his kin in evil-doing as in well?

The old man said nothing of this till the morning; but, as his purpose grew, he waxed more kind, sending one for firewood and another for milk, and a third to find lodging for our beasts. The air was pungent with wood-smoke, and so laden with the ammoniac reek of the Augean stable, that the fumes from the drying garments of a dozen unwashed men could scarcely offend. A

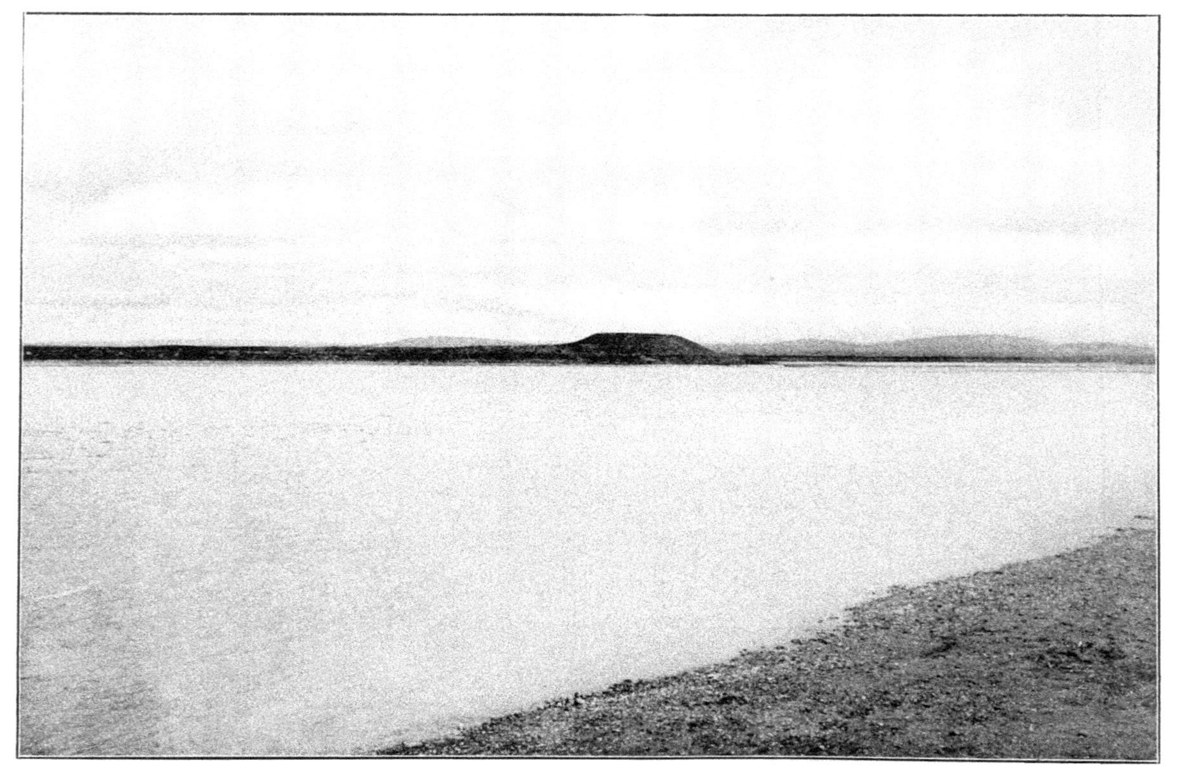

TELL AHMAR ACROSS EUPHRATES.

Facing p. 171.

sudden blaze from a fresh tuft of waxy thorn would light up the depths of the lower barn, and show us for a moment our room-mates, a steaming throng of buffaloes, oxen, sheep and goats: but it was not till we wished to sleep in the small hours that we began to hear the intermittent ruckling of a camel. In the dawn there he loomed, nearest of all the menagerie, chawing and blowing forth his froth. Poor prisoned beast! We looked at the single low door. Nothing of stature within many inches of his could pass that way. How had he got in, and how could he go out? The old sheikh threw no light on a problem which he seemed unable to appreciate, and we were left to suppose his camel had led a cloistered existence ever since he was found on some fine morning to have grown in the night the little more that would mean so much.

The morning broke fair, if not fine. Our host, who had opened his heart at last, took shadowy promises and solid silver with equal zest, and sent his blessing with us as we rode towards a white bluff honeycombed with ancient tombs, beyond whose butt a great water gleamed. Hollow echoes awoke in the cliff, half a dozen eagles flapped from their eyries, and we beheld Euphrates once more. Three or four mounds broke the eastern line of horizon, of which the nearest, rising from the river's edge, was that Tell Ahmar, where we were to seek the "writing like nails."

Euphrates is not passed, however, in one hour or in two. For all our shouting and firing of guns the two ferry boats lay motionless specks under the farther bank till almost noon-day, and we had ample time to gaze at the promised land from far. Gradually a little company formed about us, made up in part of Aleppine passengers, who had come down in two waggons to the ferry, in part of roamers from the neighbouring hills, who spied unfamiliar tents. A swarthy Bedawi sauntered up, seated himself, saluted and said, "I have nothing. With two hundred piastres I shall buy cattle." "God give you!" I remarked, "why say you so to me?" "You have them, and I have not," he replied simply. He gave place to the strange figure of a very old man, almost blind, who wore a silken coat of polychrome patchwork and a green turban, and had the delicate face and soft beard that one often sees among dervishes. The company murmured he was mad, but received him reverently, and one who was sick bowed while the thin lips muttered a prayer or charm over his head. This patriarch, also, wanted piastres. Allah had shown him in sleep the hiding-place of a great treasure, and for a little money the rich *pashas* might share the secret. Two days later we passed him digging beside a great boulder a mile down stream, but we had bought no right to share the gold he should find.

At last we descried twin high-pooped arks crawling upstream under the farther bank, each towed by a dozen straining men. In an hour they would cast off, and by grace of bare poles, unwieldy rudders, currents and eddies, cunningly used, hit our point on the shore or miss it by a hundred yards, by a quarter of a mile, by more or by less, as Allah should will. Eight times I have crossed Euphrates in flood, and eight times failed to see earthly cause why the ferry-boat should ever attain the farther shore. Once cast off, I have lost all sense of headway, and seemed to slide down a boiling race, which had the boat at its mercy, keeping pace at its sides; and thus I have drifted into mid-stream. Then

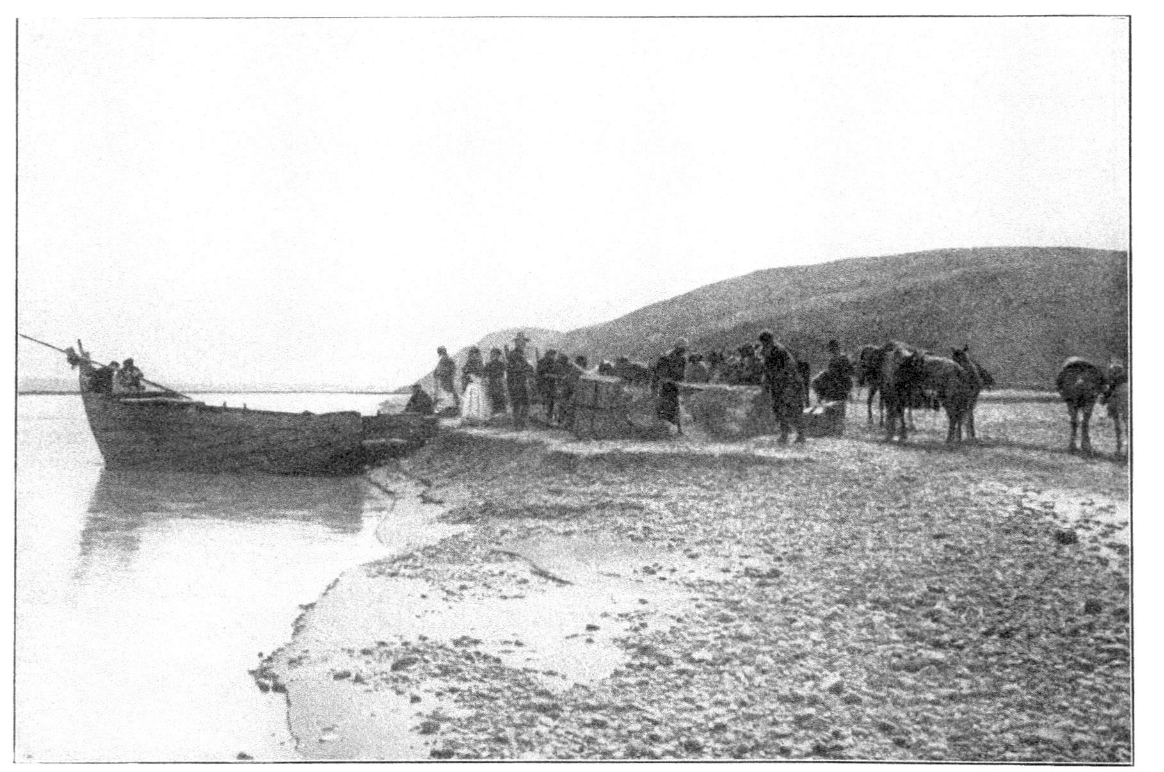

A EUPHRATEAN FERRY.

Facing p. 173.

suddenly there is great shouting and working of the huge tiller to and fro, and behold the shore itself, rushing to the rescue, crashes on the keel and the boat heels over with a groan. When I find my feet again in the swaying bilge, I perceive, amazed, that I have crossed Euphrates.

We landed at the foot of the Tell itself, and climbed it forthwith. Its flat top proved small and bare of ancient stones; but a few basalt blocks lay pell-mell at the bottom of a deep cut in its flank, and on the plain below a faintly outlined horseshoe of walls could be descried, whose horns touched the river some distance to west and east of the Tell. Within the western horn lay a few struggling huts, among which we entered the ferry-master's, to eat bread and learn what we might: but for a long while we learned nothing. Those who sat gravely round the low divan were, in the main, wayfarers like ourselves, come to take the ferry to-night or to-morrow, and the two or three natives, who came and went in the house, professed ignorance of all written or sculptured stones. At last I sent our Syrian servant outside to talk, for it was plain the peasants would not know what we wanted till they knew who we were. He went no farther, I believe, than the shady side of the hut, but in half an hour he re-entered with a man who would show a stone. We rose and followed scarcely twenty paces, and there, full in the open, lay a black slab, worn and polished by use as a seat or stand, but still faintly relieved by two sculptured figures shod with the peculiar Hittite boot. Bakshish changed hands; whispers passed round; and the guide remembered another stone, which he said was "written."

He led us north-westward out of the village, towards a gap in the long low mounds which hide the silted ruin of the city wall, and went on for a hundred yards more to the crown of a low rise. There he stayed, and, coming up with him, we saw half a dozen fragments of black basalt, which bore raised Hittite pictographs, and some part of a sculptured scene in which figured a great gross bull. The finders had broken the stone, the guide said, but found no gold within. There used to be another fragment, but where it might be now he knew not. We saw that the well-preserved pictographs were in the fine style of Carchemish, and more in number than on any one Hittite monument yet discovered, and knew that we had not come in vain to Tell Ahmar. To get due record of the monument, however, would be the work of hours. The sun was westering, and idlers, who had followed our tracks, spoke of yet other stones, and especially of "lions, written not thus, but otherwise—like nailmarks." To-morrow the camp could come over, but we must see those lions to-night.

The men led us back by the corner of the hamlet, and stopped near the river bank at a heavy block, on whose upturned face were carved two winged horses supporting the sacred palm-tree. We did what we could with camera and pencil, and then followed the guides inland across the ancient site towards a conspicuous gap in the northern wall-mounds. Through this, we were told, passed the waggon-track to Urfa, and a group of tumbled stones half seen beyond the gate raised our hopes. Nor were they to be disappointed. There lay two great winged lions of heavy Assyrian style, each inscribed with a long cuneiform text on his inner flank. The one was complete in all his parts but

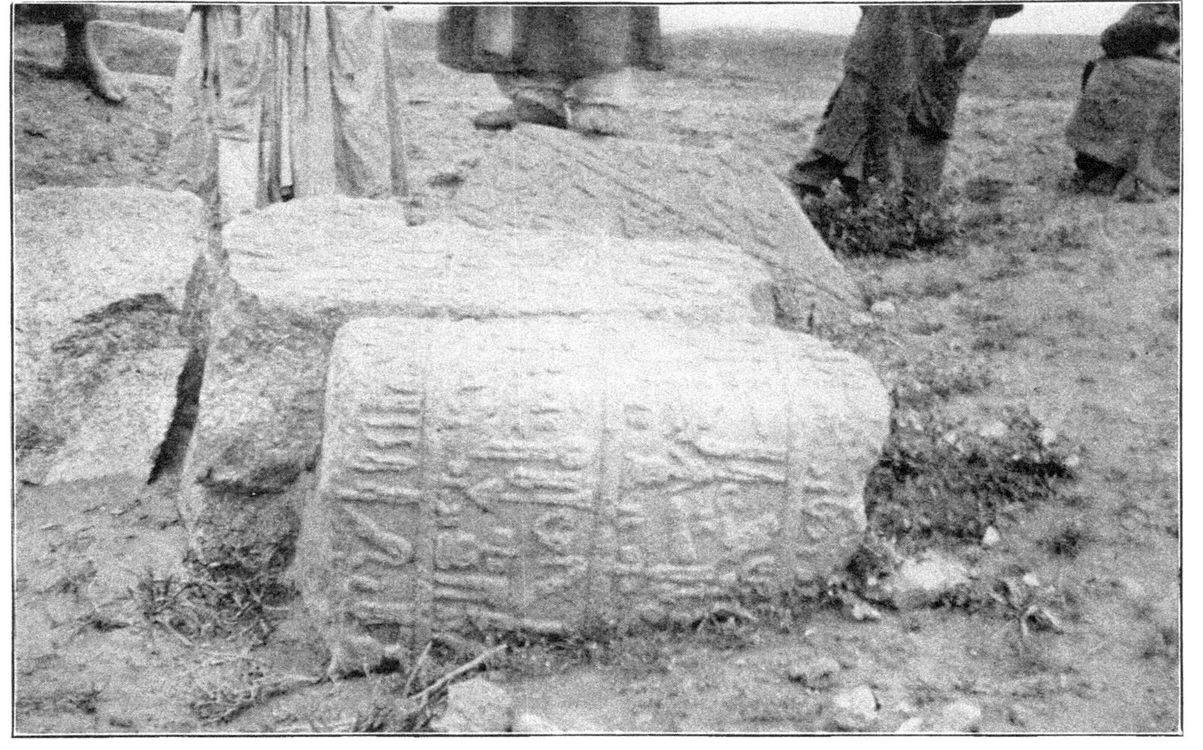

HITTITE INSCRIPTION AT TELL AHMAR.

Facing p. 174.

FALLEN LION OF SHALMANESER II. AT TELL AHMAR.

Facing p. 175.

broken in two, the other was in one piece, but without his head: when erect, each had stood nearly ten feet high from claw to crest, looking up the road towards Nineveh. Their inscriptions are of Shalmaneser the Second, the Great King of the ninth century B.C. who crossed Euphrates from Til-Barsip to Carchemish and Pitru.

Yet another monument was shown to us that evening —a broken *stela*, representing a king or god, some nine feet high, accepting the homage of a puny adorer; and three more, beside a score of little objects, cylinders and seals, both Hittite and Assyrian, we were to see on the morrow.

We tramped a mile up stream, and were poled across Euphrates again under the sunset, prize-winners in the lottery of antiquarian discovery. For we had lighted on no mean city, forgotten by Euphrates. Though passed seventy years ago by the British navigators of the river, it had been visited by no western scholar till our lucky star led us down the Sajur. What city it was and how named, its own cuneiform inscriptions do not say. Was it that Til Barsip, chief stronghold of "Ahuni, son of Adini," which Shalmaneser renamed Kar-Shalman-asharid, and made a royal residence for himself? Or, if this be placed rightly by scholars at Birejik, was one of Ahuni's lesser cities built at Tell Ahmar? This much is sure—that in Shalmaneser's day there was a city of Mesopotamia, facing the Sajur mouth, larger in area than Carchemish, where both the Hittite and the cuneiform characters were known and used; and that diggers will search there some day for the bilingual text which shall unlock the last secrets of the Hittite script.

Dark fell starlit and still by the river. The curious loungers of the daytime withdrew presently to their caves and huts on the western hills, and left us to solitary vigil. Even our muleteers, fearful for their beasts, returned at nightfall to the doubtful shelter of Avshariyeh, and the heavy silence about us was broken by nothing but the thunderous splashes, which told of Euphrates at his age-long Sisyphean task, taking from that bank to add to this. I lay uneasy with a slight fever caught yesternight, and the strong murmur of the river troubled my dreams. I seemed to drift helpless by shores that came no nearer, in a strange company of mitred men with square, curled beards, and stunt, long-nosed folk with tiptilted shoes. Then, without landing, I would find myself ashore between winged lions scanning elusive shifting symbols; but ever, before I read them, I was spirited back to the stream, and struggling among trousered bowmen to reach a bank piled with battlements and high, square towers. Suddenly the waters shrank below the boat, and the archer host rushed past me; and through a confused noise of battle and stamping hoofs, there rang in my ears a cry, "And the sixth angel poured out his vial upon the great river Euphrates; and the water thereof was dried up that the way of the Kings of the East might be prepared." Whereupon I woke to find our mules trampling about the tents in the dawn, while their drivers bandied loud words with a knot of Turcomans, who were claiming the grass by the river bank; and the sun rose on the mean mud walls of Tell Ahmar out of an empty stream.

GLASGOW: PRINTED AT THE UNIVERSITY PRESS BY ROBERT MACLEHOSE AND CO. LTD.

HITTITE PROBLEMS AND THE EXCAVATION OF CARCHEMISH

By D. G. HOGARTH

FELLOW OF THE ACADEMY

Read Dec. 13, 1911

The reasons which have led the authorities of the British Museum, and would lead any one else interested in ancient history, to promote the excavation of a first-rate Hittite site in Syria are very briefly these. The two Syrian sites, producing remains of Hittite character, which have been partially dug, viz. Sinjerli and Sakjegözü, have not yet yielded Hittite inscriptions at all, nor any other good evidence of having been inhabited by genuinely Hittite populations; yet it is on a Syrian site that there should be the best chance of finding inscriptions couched both in Hittite and in cuneiform characters, for the benefit of two populations which lived side by side but used different tongues. The nearer a site is to the Euphrates, the better are the chances of the discovery of such a bilingual text.

Further, even if the Hittite inscriptions should remain unread, the excavation of a very old stratified site, occupied at some period or periods by Hittites, must throw light on the obscure history of this people south of Taurus. Were they settled in Syria before the great descent of the Cappadocian Hatti which we now know to have taken place in the reign of Subbiluliuma, early in the fourteenth century B. C.? Hittites invaded Babylonia more than 300 years earlier than this. Were these Syrian or Cappadocian Hatti? What of the latter also after the great descent? Did they occupy Syria or merely conquer it? Its civilization certainly became Hittite; but were the Syrians who used this civilization all or any of them Hittites? What was the ethnic relation of the Hatti to the Mitanni, and what became of them and their civilization after the fall of Carchemish in 717 B. C.? Foreign influences acted upon both Hatti folk and Hatti civilization to the south of the Taurus, which did not act so strongly or at all to the north of that range. What were these, and how great was their influence? Was there a counter influence of the Hittite civilization on alien peoples? In a word, what part, if any, did the Hittites play in the general development of European civilization out of Asiatic? To answer these and similar historical questions we must first learn a great deal more about that almost unknown thing, Hittite archaeology. The commoner and the smaller Hittite products, such as the pottery, terra-cottas, weapons, have never been studied in the light of excavation evidence; yet these, by their wide diffusion and frequent occurrence, should have as much to tell us as the architecture or sculpture or written documents, and often more. If we are ignorant of the common apparatus of Hittite life, we are even more in the dark about Hittite customs in death. No Hittite graves had been found and explored before last spring. In short, Hittite archaeology has been hitherto entirely embryonic.

In the hope of new light on historical and archaeological problems, which become every day more interesting and more important with the progress of exploration in Asia Minor, the British Museum resumed last spring the excavations at Jerablus in North Syria, which it had begun on a small scale more than thirty years ago. These excavations are to be continued in the coming season. Therefore anything said now of their results must be purely provisional. But already it may be legitimate to forecast some conclusions to which they tend.

The site called the Kaleh, i. e. the castle of Jerablus or Jerabis, situated on the right bank of the Euphrates, about sixty miles north-east of Aleppo, has long been known for its comparatively great size, and for the height of the mound which represents its acropolis and for the bulk of its fortifications. There is no other ancient site on either bank of the river of such obvious importance until Babylon is reached some 500 miles down-stream,[1] and it is therefore natural that Jerablus should be identified with the principal ancient city which is known to have stood actually on the right bank of the middle Euphrates. This is the Gargamis of the Assyrian records, the Carchemish of the Old Testament.[2] Here was the capital of a kingdom always referred to as Hittite by the Ninevite scribes from at least the twelfth century B. C., and always a principal objective of the military expeditions which were pushed across the river into what the same scribes habitually called Hatti Land, viz. North and Eastern Syria. They refer, however, to other sites and tribal capitals in North Syria, and there is no evidence to show that Carchemish, when attacked by Assyria, had any lordship over these tribes and capitals, and still less that, as the capital of a Hittite province, it remained politically dependent on the Hittite realm in Cappadocia. Every-

[1] See Miss G. L. Bell, *Amurath to Amurath*, p. 33.

[2] See W. Max Müller, *Asien und Europa*, p. 263; Delitzsch, *Wo lag das Paradies?* p. 265; J. Menant, *Kar-kemish*, in *Mem. Acad. Insc.*, xxxii.

thing, on the contrary, goes to suggest that from at latest the twelfth century B.C. it was the self-dependent capital of a community isolated from the Cappadocian Hatti, though probably it had been once dependent on them. In fact it was a detached survival of the empire established by the Cappadocian Hatti in Syria early in the fourteenth century B.C., of which the Boghaz Keui archives (as well as those of El Amarna in Egypt) have informed us. The cuneiform records further reveal that Carchemish was a strong place with a high acropolis rising immediately from the river, that on several occasions it yielded rich spoil, and that it had sufficient commercial importance to give its name to a measure of weight called the *maneh* or *mina* of Carchemish. The discovery of monuments in Hittite artistic style, accompanied by Hittite inscriptions, during the slight excavations made at the spot between 1876 and 1880 by the British Museum, practically confirmed the identification of Jerablus with Carchemish,[1] and, although even now no absolute proof has come to hand, that identification may safely be assumed.

The site may be considered in two parts: (1) the great Acropolis mound, and (2) the Lower City. The latter consists of an oval area fenced landwards by a great horseshoe wall between whose horns the acropolis rises from the river. The oval covers about three-quarters of a square mile, and its fortifications are pierced by two main gates on the south-west and south-east. Outside these gates roads can be traced with tombs beside them, and also remains of an outer circumvallation, which probably enclosed dwellings of poorer folk excluded from the royal city. But since no excavation has been done in this outer area, we need consider at present only the inner royal city, with its acropolis.

Let me take the acropolis first, although this is to invert the geographical order in which we actually dug. The great flat-topped citadels which rise out of Hittite sites in Syria have long called for thorough examination. Their summit plateaux, if they bear any ruins of structures at all, generally show Byzantine, early Moslem, or even Frankish remains, and Carchemish is no exception, for it shows Byzantine mixed with later Arab. But on many such mounds Hittite stones have been extracted from the flanks, e.g. at Tell Ahmar and Kellekli. The question to be solved at Jerablus was whether a Hittite fortress had stood on this mound but had either been removed by later builders or been buried by the accumulation

[1] See Wright, *Empire of the Hittites*, pp. 63 and 143; and W. H. Rylands in *Trans. Soc. Bibl. Arch.*, viii. 3. No report of the actual excavation has ever been published.

of dust and later remains. If the latter was the case, then at what level had it stood? How deep did human remains descend in the bowels of this great mass about 150 feet in height and a quarter of a mile in length?

In the past season, in short, we had first to find out by cuttings the magnitude of our task. Had we to remove a mountain in order to get at the Hittite level, or was there a rock core rising so high in the heart of the mound that the earliest remains might lie not so very deep down after all?

This problem was not to be wholly solved in the first season. The later structures on the acropolis proved to have left a very deep deposit, and the work went slowly owing to frequent interruptions by terrible afternoon winds which sweep down the Euphrates valley in spring, raising such whirlwinds of dust that digging has to be suspended on exposed spots. But considerable progress towards the solution was made by means of headings, driven into the steep slope falling to the river where the winds have prevented much accumulation, and also by deep shafts sunk from the summit and in some cases opened into the headings so as to become cross trenches. Thus it was found that on the southern and broadest end of this mound there had been built in the Roman Syrian epoch a great structure, probably a temple, in the style of Baalbec, based on a solid platform, whose foundations went down nearly thirty feet through masses of unburnt brickwork. This structure must belong to the earlier period of re-occupation which is represented by the superficial remains in the lower city. No sign of a Hittite building appeared at this end of the acropolis, but nearer the centre, where the temple platform had not extended, crude brickwork had survived not more than four feet down. This appears to be remains of an Assyrian structure, probably of the eighth century B.C. But the diggers were unable to get below its great mass and therefore no Hittite structure was reached here (though a few fragments of Hittite sculpture were found), and it is clear that without enormous labour and expenditure it cannot be explored if it does exist. In the lowest level of a heading driven into this end of the mound from the river slope, however, and about fifty feet perpendicularly below the summit, the outcrop of a horizontal stratum was tapped which contained implements of very white obsidian, such as comes from the Caucasus, and of flint. With these were sherds of pottery, both pebble-polished and painted, but wheel-made, and beads and other small objects in rock-crystal and polished stones. Though representing a primitive settlement these objects can hardly have belonged to the very earliest inhabitants of Carchemish; nor was virgin earth anywhere touched. It looks, therefore, as though the original dome of the rock lies more than fifty feet below the present summit of the mound—a fact which renders thorough exploration of the earliest level of human settlement here practically impossible, although its outcrop may yet be reached by lateral headings.

At the other end of the acropolis, however, i. e. the northern, which is narrower and can be cut through more quickly, the prospect is better. Here there has been no massive late structure, but merely a complex of mean rooms without deep foundations. Eighteen feet below are remains of a roughly-built stone fortification, and almost immediately under this again was found a well-built course of walling, resting on solid foundations; some of its blocks are dressed with such slightly convex faces as characterize masonry uncovered in the lower town and dated to the later Hittite age by the sculptures and other objects found in association or at the same level. The diggers in the past spring were able only to lay bare one short stretch of this wall at the bottom of a very deep trench; but they were fortunate enough to find close to it two remarkable Hittite monuments, a column-base flanked by two lions, and a very well preserved altar-stela inscribed with a linear Hittite inscription. These monuments seem to have been overthrown and abandoned at the same epoch as the neighbouring wall, and they go far to confirm the excavators' impression that they have here determined the position of a fortress or palace of the latest Hittite period.

The discovery of the two monuments just mentioned, which are of unusually fine work and true Hittite, offers good hope that something more than a mere ground plan will ultimately be recovered here. The palace was perhaps restored and reused after 717 B.C. by the Assyrian conqueror, Sargon III, one of whose bricks was found hard by.

The acropolis was not only a fortress at various stages of its growth, but also during a certain period a cemetery. The number of burials which have been brought to light is surprising when the small area of surface actually probed is considered. There are three different kinds of graves; but since the bodies in all these appear to have been cut up in the same way before interment and the pottery associated with them is always of the same peculiar kind, the dead buried in all three kinds of graves must have differed not in race or period, but only in social circumstances. The poorest were buried in earth and their huddled remains were covered by basins of coarse red or buff ware. These graves seldom or never have any furniture.

The next grade is pot burial, the jars used being about two feet long and of slender form with narrow mouth.[1] Placed beside the coffin

[1] Cp. Report of Cornell Expedition, *Travels and Studies*, I. ii, p. 23.

jar but never inside it were found in several instances small vases of the shape of a champagne glass, whose bowl and foot were wheel-made while their hollow connecting stems had been shaped by hand. Very rarely are these vases painted, and the few exceptions show simple geometrically disposed lines in matt red on buff ground. Apart from the graves fragments of this ware were so rarely found on any part of the site, that it seems possible it was a peculiar fabric used only for funerary purposes.

The best graves, however, were oblong cists, walled and roofed with stone slabs. Only four of these came to light, the largest being one which I cleared out with my own hands. It contained three dissected skeletons, nearly fifty large 'champagne-glass' and other vases, some bronze pins, many tiny glazed beads, fallen from necklaces, and a small bronze axe-head of plain wedge shape with straight cutting edge and no shaft hole. Bronze knives and many pins were obtained from other cists. These graves occurred in the flanks of the acropolis up to only twelve feet below its present summit. They must, therefore, have been made when that summit was not greatly lower than now; but since they contained no trace of iron, but did contain bronze, they are to be dated as far back at least as the Assyrian occupation. One, however, occurred under the foundation exposed at the north end of the mound which has been already described and conjectured to be late Hittite. On this account, as well as on account of the bronze types found in the cist-graves, I incline to regard all these burials as of the full Hittite period, probably of the eleventh or twelfth century B.C.

If so they are the first Hittite graves which so far have been explored anywhere and are of great archaeological interest. The graves found by von Luschan at Sinjerli (on the Palace mound) were not certainly Hittite. Indeed one may doubt whether Sinjerli was occupied by Hatti at all. All its inscriptions are Cuneiform or Aramaic, and its art appears to be of a derived type, not true Hittite.

There remains to be described the more extensive work done by us below the acropolis on the landward side. It was far more productive of archaeological spoil than that just described, but, to my mind, it promises less, for its results tend to show that the acropolis was the only part of the site inhabited until a comparatively late period—until, at earliest, the coming of the Hatti from Cappadocia in the fourteenth century B.C. At any rate the original Carchemish, known to the Egyptians of the eighteenth dynasty, was a much smaller place, perched on the mound above the river, and under its ruins only can we hope to recover the primaeval history of pre-Hittite Syria. What has been done so far in the lower city is this in brief. A great stone stairway, at the landward foot of the southern end of the acropolis, had been found by the diggers of thirty years ago, but not completely cleared. They seem also to have explored very partially certain ruins of structures lying to the north of this stairway. From these ruins, but chiefly from the sides of the stairway itself, they extracted the inscribed and other monuments now in the British Museum. We reopened the stairway, which had become covered again with débris, and found that it rose by twenty-one shallow steps from a court, paved with pebbles, to a much ruined platform; but so far as we can find it did not continue beyond this towards the acropolis, nor to any building lying directly in its own axis.

If so it must have given access to some other building, probably a palace or temple, lying to one side of it, and the researches of our predecessors and our own later trenching suggest that such a building lay to the left or north. But how far it extended and what its character was we are not yet in a position to say. Part of it seems to lie very deep. A trial pit sunk a short distance north of the stair went down nearly twenty-four feet and then hit the top of a good ashlar wall. There are evidently hollows to be expected in the original superficies of the site and the virgin soil lies deeper on the northern part than on the southern.

Having cleared the stairway, we cut back landward from its foot for about thirty yards, digging down through about seventeen feet of earth to the Hittite pavement, and sinking shafts at intervals to the virgin earth. This occurred on an average not more than three feet below the pebble pavement, without any intermediate human remains, except at one point close to the stair-foot, where a pot burial of later type than those on the acropolis was found. On this part of the site, then, the lowest existing stratum has been explored; but it is not nearly so old as the lower strata of the acropolis.

In cutting back from the stair-foot we found that the pebble pavement was bounded on the north by a long wall of ashlar, faced on the south side but left rough on the north, which continued, with a slight outward slant, the line of the north edge of the stair. After continuing about eighty feet to the west this returned northward, but we had not time to follow it far. The roughness of the ashlar facing on the inner side of the angle so formed precludes the idea that we had here turned a corner of the palace or temple lying north of the stairway. This must begin farther east, and a small door which opens off the stair itself into a paved court must be one way of approach to it. Time did not permit the thorough exploration of this building; but some trials were made within its probable area, both at the south-western angle and elsewhere, and a well-built but much ruined chamber was cleared, the masonry of which is of the late Hittite type. The walling of the little court opening off the stairway was evidently lined with glazed and coloured bricks, of which several were found fallen.

Into the long lower wall seems to have been built a series of large reliefs, which faced outwards to the paved court. We found them fallen into the court to the number of thirteen in all. Six of these represent war chariots in action; two, warriors on foot; four, monstrous divine figures; and one, occurring about the middle of the series, bears a long inscription in relief characters, below which appear three bearded heads and sixteen cut-off hands. As these slabs originally faced outwards, they were the lining of a monumental approach to the stairway, and led up to a series which lined the north side of the latter. One member of this series is still *in situ*, as to its lower half, and we were able to restore its upper part almost entirely from fragments found near by. Another large slab has fallen in two pieces not far away; and part of a third, which was still *in situ* thirty years ago, as the photographs taken by the Wolfe expedition and published in the American Journal of Archaeology[1] show, was recovered from the foot of the stair. Parts of others were found higher up. Similar reliefs evidently lined the opposite edge of the stair; but these had almost all been removed by the diggers between 1876 and 1880. A great carved slab at the south foot, however, defied their efforts, and still stands on its original plinth.

In excavating the considerable area occupied by the stairway, and the approach to it, we lighted on a number of inscribed and carved fragments, none of which, however, was found in its original place, but all lay at various levels in the overlying debris, as though abandoned at various periods by seekers after squared stones. About sixty out of the ninety Hittite inscriptions, which we can add to the *Corpus Inscr. Hettiticarum*, were so found. The rest, with the exception of one from the north end of the acropolis mound, and three or four discovered in other villages of the district, were picked up on the surface of the site or its immediate vicinity, or were extracted from the walls of ruined Byzantine buildings. Several reliefs, much weathered but still possible to distinguish, which had remained unnoticed by our predecessors and even by ourselves for awhile, were also found on the surface. Three of these still stand in line as though they had flanked an approach to the river round the

[1] By Hayes Ward, vol. iv, pl. 9.

southern butt of the acropolis. All have an early appearance, the style of their art seeming to owe almost nothing to Assyria, but much to Cappadocia and Babylonia. Except for trial excavations in houses built of sun-dried bricks, remains of which apparently survive all over the site, wherever protected by hollows in the original superficies, and except also for a tentative exploration of a necropolis outside the walls on the north, which resulted in the discovery of some water-logged rock-graves of post-Hittite date, this was all the digging done in the first season. I shall try to estimate very summarily and provisionally the contribution which its results make, or seem likely to make, when followed up farther, towards the solution of some problems of southern Hittite history.

On the problem of decipherment, whose solution will contribute materially to the solution of all the other problems, we have not been able, unfortunately, to throw any new light as yet. We began the excavation in strong hopes of finding Hittite records in cuneiform, if not a bilingual inscription in both the cuneiform and the Hittite scripts. Our hope will be judged reasonable enough when the geographical situation of Jerablus is considered, and it is remembered that three years before both Hittite and cuneiform monuments were discovered at Tell Ahmar, about fifteen miles down-stream, on the opposite bank of the Euphrates. This latter place we now know (since Mr. Campbell Thompson has obtained a better reading of the inscriptions on its gateway lions) to have been Til Barsip, where Assyrian kings often embarked for the passage of the river.[1] But our four months' digging at Jerablus brought no scrap of a cuneiform tablet from any part of the site, and only a few small fragments of basaltic monuments inscribed in cuneiform, of about Nebuchadnezzar's time. Our Hittite inscriptions add several new characters, and illustrate more different styles of graving than have been noticed before. But they have not made decipherment easier, and we can only go on hoping through another season.

(1) *Hittite History.*—On certain of the historical problems we shall, I think, be in a position after another three months or so of digging to throw some light. We have found that the acropolis of Carchemish is stratified down to a depth which proves inhabitation back to a remote period, long pre-Hittite. The earliest stratum which we have explored contains pottery, stone implements, &c., to which no parallels have yet been found in Cappadocia; and this stratum is evidently not the absolutely earliest on the site. We ought

[1] Delitzsch, *op. cit.*, p. 263.

by about next June to be able to say where Hittite strata end and pre-Hittite begin, and to assign rough dating.

In strata certainly Hittite we can already distinguish at least three periods in ceramic production, three in sculpture, and two, if not three, in architecture. Of the pottery, which has been carefully studied by Mr. T. E. Lawrence, the earliest Hittite types have been found on the acropolis, whose lower strata, above the obsidian-bearing stratum, contain wheel-made unslipped bowls, jugs, and urns, either unpolished, with simple geometric ornament laid on with a coarse brush in purplish black and red paint, or polished, with similar incised ornament. These precede by a long period of time the pottery in the acropolis graves, which takes several forms, the champagne glass, with a hand-made hollow stem joining wheel-made bowl and foot, predominating. All these funerary vases are unslipped and unpolished, but of finely levigated clay, and in a few instances they show simple chevrons or other geometric motives painted in red on their rims. The hand-made basins, used for the poorest burials, are contemporary with these.

Following the cist-grave vases come undecorated plates and pots in red, yellow, and buff wares, pebble-polished in vertical lines. Such are found not only on the acropolis, but also in the brick houses below, and are contemporary with the earliest and most numerous terra-cotta figurines. They were succeeded by horizontally polished wares, the burnished rings on which have been made by a sharp point while the vase was revolving on the potter's wheel. This type of ware is characteristic of the later Hittite stratum at the foot of the stairway, and is probably contemporary with the building lying to the north of the latter. It is the first ware found on the site which has also been found commonly in the Hatti area of Asia Minor. When it begins to get scarce, a rough buff ware with wavy combed ornament comes in; but this appears to be of the Assyrian age. Those who know the Cappadocian area will note the entire lack of the white slipped pottery with polychrome decoration, and the red faced pottery with black ornament, which prevail there,[1] and will wonder why it is only at a late Hittite age that Cappadocia and Syria begin to share their pot-types. I can only suggest that the Hatti of Carchemish were a small ruling class which imposed its art of sculpture on a subject population, but accepted the commoner local products.

A certain sculpture, a processional relief, which appears to stand almost in its original position at the south-eastern foot of the acropolis,

[1] See J. L. Myres, 'Early Pot Fabrics of Asia Minor,' in *Journ. Anthrop. Inst.* xxxiii.

where the accumulation of deposit above bed-rock is, for some reason—perhaps wind-erosion—very slight, is in a different style from all the rest so far found on the site, and this is, I think, an earlier style; for while it shows no Assyrian influence and only remote Babylonian, it is very close to the style of the reliefs of Eyuk, which are thought the earliest of the north Cappadocian sculptures. One would naturally ascribe this relief to a Cappadocian sculptor who had come down to Syria before the great descent of the Hatti of Boghaz Keui. Then there is a group of reliefs found in and about the monumental approach to the stairway, mostly executed in basalt, and all of finer and more individual style than the others, which are mainly of limestone. Such are a very typically Hittite god's head, with legend in relieved characters above it; a broken part of a statue with beautiful rosette ornament on its robe; and two lower parts of stelae showing marching warriors. These display some Babylonian characteristics but no Assyrian, and approximate closely to the Yasili Kaia sculptures near Boghaz Keui. Finally, there are the rest of the approach and stairway reliefs, which are strongly influenced by Assyrian art, but still distinctly Hittite.

As for the architecture, there are certainly two Hittite periods represented in the stairway and approach. The former had been laid out originally independent of the latter. One of the flanking reliefs (of earlier style) has been shifted to suit the slight angle at which the later approach meets the stair-foot, and the stairs show numerous patches and signs of reconstruction. Such reconstruction cannot, however, have been done after the Assyrian conquest, for purely Hittite sculptures were used to adorn the latest stairway. The courtyard to which the gate on the north side of the stair leads lies very high, and so does the room dug out by us to the south-west; but in a trial pit close to the latter a very much lower structure (seven metres down) was revealed. This last will be found, I prophesy, to belong to an earlier palace, and the courtyard and room with the approach and the reconstructed stairway will be relegated to a later—the earlier being of the Boghaz Keui period, i.e. fourteenth and thirteenth centuries B.C., the later of a period when Assyrian influence had become much stronger than Cappadocian in Syria, perhaps in the eleventh century.

The sum of the evidence obtained so far at Carchemish, therefore, seems to me to support the theory that there were Hittites, or at least Hittite cultural influences, in Syria before its conquest by the king of the Hatti of Boghaz Keui; that the Cappadocian occupation established by the latter did not eliminate the earlier stock at Carchemish, and was not very long-lasting; and that it was succeeded by a period of independence of Cappadocia and dependence on Assyria, prior to complete conquest by the latter. The period of Cappadocian occupation was, however, that of the city's greatest extent and power; while that of the Assyrian occupation, after Sargon's conquest in 717, was one of weakness and decay, to be followed, not by an Aramaean revival, but by virtual desolation until Graeco-Syrian times.

(2) *Character of Hittite Civilization in Syria.*—This large question involves others, of which the chief is concerned with the nature, period, and strength of the new external influences which may have come to be exerted on Hittite civilization when domiciled south of Taurus. The sculptures from the Hittite strata so far explored at Jerablus show general cultural uniformity with Hittite monuments farther north. There can be no question, not only that the Carchemish society came under direct Cappadocian influence, but also that this Cappadocian civilization was a very vigorous and independent one, when it reached Syria. The script and the manner of cutting it on hard stone are the same in Syria as in Asia Minor, and the Carchemish lapicides show from the first that sureness of hand, both in the general disposition of symbols and in the particular details of them, which could only have resulted from an artistic tradition very long established. The facial types on both the two earlier classes of monuments are identical with those of the most typical Hittite art of Asia Minor and have the same individuality. Not less identical are the poses of the figures, their dress, their attributes. So too are most of the divine representations. From near the Black Sea and the Aegean to the Middle Euphrates there was at one time one plastic art of the Hatti, expressing identical subjects in one and the same spirit and technique. But both on monuments and on lesser objects of local fabric, which are to be referred to the later Hittite period at Carchemish, one notes discrepant elements—elements, that is to say, whose origin and development are not obviously to be traced to the Hatti of Cappadocia. One alien influence is so patent in those sculptures of the Lower City which seem to belong to the approach and restored stairway, that it needs no proof except such as three or four illustrations will afford. This is the *Assyrian.* The Chariot reliefs, the great slab still *in situ* at the south foot of the stairs (bearing, be it noted, Hittite symbols), the bearded bull-footed figures upholding sacred palm-trees, and the great slab inscribed in Hittite, but showing also three bearded heads and sixteen hands, are as Assyrian as they can be, while remaining clearly Hittite work.

There is nothing known to me among the Hittite monuments of Asia Minor so Assyrian as any of these sculptures.

Among what may be considered Mesopotamian importations into the southern Hittite country, special attention should be called to the religious ones. I have said above that there is much in common between the religious representations of the Cappadocian Hatti and those of the Syrian; but there are also differences. The chief is the presence of the nude goddess in the south. The Jerablus relief, on which she appears before a throned king, near whose head is a Hittite inscription, has been known for thirty years, but now for the first time we are able to publish good photographs of its severed parts. The Cappadocian goddesses are generally seated and always draped. Other non-Cappadocian divine figures at Jerablus are the bearded bull-footed demons who grasp the stems of palm-trees. Both these and the nude goddess have well-known Mesopotamian prototypes, and it is obviously from the east that they have come into the Hittite theology.

If Assyrian influence was to be expected, so too was another, the *Egyptian*. But actual evidence of the latter is somewhat lacking on the Carchemish site. A handful of amulets in Egyptian glazed clay, and apparently not of earlier period than the Saitic, alone among objects discovered by us represent commodities of the Nile. I cannot trace direct Egyptian influence on any of the Hittite sculptures found so far at Carchemish, early or late, and very little that can have come indirectly viâ Assyria. This fact, however, must not be insisted upon after only one season's digging.

There are also, in my opinion, indications of another foreign influence, which I should trace ultimately to the Aegean civilization in its latest Bronze Age period, but proximately to Cyprus. I prefer not to deal in detail with these until more of those smaller objects, which usually illustrate foreign influences better than the larger, have been found, and I will only call attention now to two phenomena. First, the crested helmets of the warriors on two slabs from the Approach —helmets such as a steatite filler-vase from Hagia Triada proves were known in Late Minoan Crete. Second, the curious 'champagne-glass' vases from the Acropolis graves, for which I find it difficult to account without presuming indebtedness to some alien model. The form should belong to a late stage of ceramic art, which has always been slow to evolve a foot for vases, and slower to evolve a long foot. The particular form found at Jerablus has, it will be remembered, a peculiar feature, that the cup and foot are neatly wheel-made, but the connecting stem is rather clumsily shaped by hand. The potters seem to have been botching a borrowed form which was somewhat beyond their powers. If so, what was their model? Mr. H. R. Hall has suggested to me that the carinated form of the bowl and the small foot recall certain Egyptian *alabastra*; but I cannot find any convincing Egyptian prototype, although he is probably right in seeing resemblance between some other vases, found with the 'champagne-glass' vases, and Ramesside forms. Nor can I find a Mesopotamian prototype. The nearest and most accessible region which was producing a 'champagne-glass' vase round about 1100 B.C. was the Aegean in the last period of the Bronze Age. Such vases, though of much finer fabric, having bowls not carinated, and bearing ear-handles, have been found at several points on the western coast of Asia Minor and in Rhodes and Cyprus. It is not a very far cry thence to North Syria; and I suggest provisionally that the Jerablus potters in the latest Bronze Age were trying clumsily to cater for a fashion which had been set by the Aegean at a very slightly earlier period of the same age.

Such a connexion is not difficult to credit, nor is it now suggested for the first time. There are several classes of Hittite antiquities found in Syria (though not yet at Jerablus) which have already been held to suggest the passing of artistic types and influence from the Mediterranean to North Syria and vice versa. Such are the Syrian bronze cult figurines with high peaked caps which in dress and pose recall Aegean statuettes, for example, a silver figurine from Nezero in Thessaly, now in the Ashmolean. On these Prof. W. N. Bates's article in the American Journal of Archaeology (1911, No. 1) should be consulted. Such too are many of the Hittite seal types.

On the other hand, there is also a good deal of Cypriote evidence for a connexion between Cyprus, after it had received an Aegean, probably Cretan, immigration about 1300 B.C., and the south Hittite area. Cypriote pottery or local ware repeating Cypriote ornament has come to light in all the three excavations conducted on north Syrian Hittite sites, viz. at Sinjerli, Sakjegözü, and Jerablus; and if north Syrian Hittite ware has not been noticed yet in Cyprus, its lack may be explained by the fact that, up to the present, no one has known enough about this ware to be able to detect it. Several objects in the Salaminian treasure of Enkomi, the date of whose burial falls in about the last century of the second millennium, have long been recognized as giving proof of Asiatic influence which was ultimately Mesopotamian, but had filtered through some medium, presumably north Syrian; and, especially, a correspondence has been pointed out between the hunting scenes carved respectively on the ivory casket of Enkomi and the slabs from Sakjegözü, now in Berlin. The curious Cypriote cylinder seals, too, have been accounted for in the same way, and there are other classes of seals which suggest connexion between Cyprus and the Hittite country. For example, a claw-handled seal in gold, found in a tomb at the ancient Tamasos in Cyprus, shows the same peculiar decorative elements in its ornate borders as distinguish the so-called 'Half-Bead' seals, i. e. hemispheroids, which often bear legends in Hittite characters. One of these hemispheroids in the Ashmolean collection is inscribed in what is almost certainly a primitive Cypriote script; while another seal also of typically Hittite form, a flattened spheroid, which is in the same collection, bears a legend in Cypriote characters.

For EU product safety concerns, contact us at Calle de José Abascal, 56–1°, 28003 Madrid, Spain or eugpsr@cambridge.org.

www.ingramcontent.com/pod-product-compliance
Ingram Content Group UK Ltd.
Pitfield, Milton Keynes, MK11 3LW, UK
UKHW010343140625
459647UK00010B/784

* 9 7 8 1 1 0 8 0 4 1 9 2 8 *